AN INTRODUCTION TO REPO MARKETS

Third Edition

The Securities & Investment Institute

Mission Statement:

To set standards of professional excellence and integrity for the investment and securities industry, providing qualifications and promoting the highest level of competence to our members, other individuals and firms.

The Securities and Investment Institute is the UK's leading professional and membership body for practitioners in the securities and investment industry, with more than 16,000 members with an increasing number working outside the UK. It is also the major examining body for the industry, with a full range of qualifications aimed at people entering and working in it. More than 30,000 examinations are taken annually in more than 30 countries.

You can contact us through our website *www.sii.org.uk*

Our membership believes that keeping up to date is central to professional development. We are delighted to endorse the Wiley/SII publishing partnership and recommend this series of books to our members and all those who work in the industry.

Ruth Martin
Managing Director

AN INTRODUCTION TO REPO MARKETS

Third Edition

. . . .

Moorad Choudhry

with a contribution from Daniel Franks

JOHN WILEY & SONS, LTD

Published in 2006 by John Wiley & Sons Ltd, The Atrium, Southern Gate, Chichester,
West Sussex PO19 8SQ, England

Telephone (+44) 1243 779777

Email (for orders and customer service enquiries): cs-books@wiley.co.uk
Visit our Home Page on www.wiley.com

Other Wiley Editorial Offices

John Wiley & Sons, Inc., 111 River Street, Hoboken, NJ 07030, USA

Jossey-Bass, 989 Market Street, San Francisco, CA 94103-1741, USA

Wiley-VCH Verlag GmbH, Boschstr. 12, D-69469 Weinheim, Germany

John Wiley & Sons Australia Ltd, 42 McDougall Street, Milton, Queensland 4064, Australia

John Wiley & Sons (Asia) Pte Ltd, 2 Clementi Loop #02-01, Jin Xing Distripark, Singapore 129809

John Wiley & Sons Canada Ltd, 22 Worcester Road, Etobicoke, Ontario, Canada M9W 1L1

Wiley also publishes its books in a variety of electronic formats. Some content that appears
in print may not be available in electronic books.

British Library Cataloguing in Publication Data

A catalogue record for this book is available from the British Library

ISBN-13 978-0-470-01756-2 (PB)

Project management by Originator, Gt Yarmouth, Norfolk (typeset in 10/12pt Trump Mediaeval).
Printed and bound in Great Britain by T.J. International Ltd, Padstow, Cornwall.
This book is printed on acid-free paper responsibly manufactured from sustainable forestry
in which at least two trees are planted for each one used for paper production.

To Nick Procter
I think we all want to be you ...

CONTENTS

. . . .

FOREWORD

. . . .

Repo has the widest application of almost any instrument within the financial markets. The market provides financing efficiencies, yield enhancement, liquidity, price discovery and transparency to a broad array of asset classes, from the highly commoditised to the esoteric. The liquidity and flexibility of repo attracts a wide cross section of participants, including commercial and investment banks, asset managers and corporate treasurers.

Financial institutions lending their assets via repo achieve enhanced portfolio returns through lower financing rates and volatility than the unsecured cash market. Investors needing to place cash holdings can precisely tailor their requirements through repo, taking advantage of its security, flexibility and most importantly its simplicity. As a money market instrument, repo enables market participants to express views on short-term interest rates, collateral types, specific issuers and bond issues. Repo is a major component in the Fixed Income market, as the key determinant in pricing underlying assets, particularly in hedging and in correctly trading the basis between on- and off-balance sheet instruments in the government, corporate and asset-backed bond and derivatives markets.

Exponential growth in volumes, evolving scope and its huge importance in the efficient functioning of debt capital markets necessitate a wider understanding of the product. Repo differentiates itself from other financial products in that practitioners need to have a robust understanding of the linkages between the underlying asset and the corresponding credit, regulatory, accounting, and legal and settlement risks.

In this highly readable text Moorad Choudhry provides the essential account of the repo market that will appeal to student, academic and market practitioner alike. The book assumes no prior knowledge;

with the early stages providing a comprehensive primer, using practical examples drawn from his extensive trading experience across repo, bond and structured products. The book considers further applications of repo, underlining its importance across the dealing room of financial institutions.

The reader's attention is focused on the benefits of repo throughout, combining annotated technical analysis with real world application. The accessible style provides an indispensable guide for anyone with an interest in repo and the money markets. The book is set apart by giving the reader a broad awareness of the connectivity between repo and the wider range of capital markets businesses.

Adam Sutton
Head of European Repo
Global Funding Desk (Europe)
Bank of America

PREFACE

. . . .

The world of fixed income is dynamic and ever-changing, with new instruments, applications and processes being developed all the time. Although it is a commoditised and standardised product of long standing, repo, short for 'sale and *repurchase* agreement', is no different and we have new variations on a theme to talk about in this updated third edition. The devil is in the detail, as countless unimaginative journalists like to say, and the new developments in repo since the first edition of this book was published in 1999 are mainly of a detailed nature. As we said, repo is in essence a standardised product, as well as a very simple and basic one; this means it is easily adapted to new applications in new markets.

Another thing one would hope has been adapted and improved is my writing. It would be a poor author, in any field, whose quality of writing style and delivery had not improved over a period of seven years, so this third edition incorporates some additional bells and whistles to convince you that its purchase was worthwhile! What do we have that is new? Worked examples are now illustrated with Bloomberg screens, which most readers can expect to come across whether they are at a bank or indeed in the finance or economics department of their university. Other new content for this third edition includes:

- basket repo funding of portfolios of assets;
- illustrations of repo for structured finance securities such as asset-backed securities;
- synthetic repo or total return swaps, both single-name and basket deals;
- use of repo in commercial paper conduit structures;
- an updated look at the standard repo agreement, the GMRA, written by Daniel Franks;
- new illustrations from different markets.

For students and those taking training courses we also have some introductory-level exercises and a case study that illustrates the basic concepts.

We have removed the separate chapter on emerging market repo; the instrument itself is not a different one simply because one is dealing in an emerging market, even though local customs and practices may differ. Higher risk associated with emerging market collateral is also managed using the same practices adopted in developed markets. Hence, we don't feel the need to address these markets separately. Practitioners who need to get to grips with a specific country market will need to research this themselves! Also, we don't pretend to be able to cover the nuances of legal and accounting issues associated with repo so this is introduced in overview manner only.

As before, this book is intended for beginners or newcomers to the subject so we keep the level accessible at all times.

Enjoy!

Moorad Choudhry
Surrey, England
March 2006

PREFACE TO
THE FIRST EDITION

· ·

The repo market is an important component of the global capital and money markets. The first repo transactions were initiated by the US Federal Reserve over eighty years ago, since which time repo has become the main instrument of open market operations for many major central banks around the world. The market has grown substantially in the last ten years and is now estimated to account for up to 50% of daily settlement activity in non-US government bonds world-wide; this is a phenomenal figure. Daily outstanding volume in international repo transactions is approximately £420 billion.

The rapid growth in the use of repo world-wide has been attributed to several factors including the rise in non-bank funding and disintermediation, the expansion of public debt, the liquidity of the instrument itself and the generally high quality of collateral used. Its flexibility has resulted in repo being taken up by a wide variety of market players, from securities houses and investment banks to fund managers, corporate treasurers and local authorities. Virtually all major currency markets in the world now have an established repo market; the facility is also increasingly used in developing currency markets as well. Trading so-called 'emerging markets' repo brings with it specific risks and requirements and these are examined in a separate section.

This book is aimed at those with little or no previous understanding of or exposure to the repo markets; however it also investigates the markets to sufficient depth to be of use to a more experienced practitioner. It is primarily aimed at front office, middle office and back office banking and fund management staff who are involved to some extent in the repo markets. Others including corporate and local authority treasurers, risk management and legal department staffs may also find the contents useful. Comments on the text should be sent to the author care of the Securities and Investment Institute.

ABOUT THE AUTHOR

Moorad Choudhry is Head of Treasury at KBC Financial Products in London. He joined there from JPMorgan Chase Bank, where he was a vice-president in Structured Finance Services sales and marketing. Prior to that he was a sterling proprietary trader in the Treasury division at Hambros Bank Limited, and at ABN Amro Hoare Govett Sterling Bonds Limited where he ran the short-dated gilts and money markets desk. He began his City career at the London Stock Exchange in 1989.

Moorad is a Visiting Professor at the Department of Economics, London Metropolitan University, a Visiting Research Fellow at the ICMA Centre, University of Reading, a Senior Fellow at the Centre for Mathematical Trading and Finance, Cass Business School, and a Fellow of the Securities and Investment Institute.

Chapter

1

....

INTRODUCTION TO REPO

The repo market is a vital element of the global capital and money markets. The first repo transactions were initiated by the US Federal Reserve in 1918, since which time repo has become the main instrument of open market operations for virtually all central banks around the world. It is also a major component of the global money markets. The market experienced substantial growth during the 1990s and is now estimated to account for up to 50% of daily settlement activity in non-US Government bonds world-wide; this is a phenomenal figure. Daily outstanding volume in international repo transactions has been estimated at between £440 billion to £450 billion; in the USD domestic market, daily deal volume is over $1,000 billion.

Repo, from 'sale and *repurchase* agreement', is closely linked to other segments of the debt and equity markets. From its use as a financing instrument for market makers to its use in the open market operations of central banks, and its place between the bond markets and the money markets, it integrates the various disparate elements of the marketplace and allows the raising of corporate finance across all sectors.

Repo is an interesting product because, although it is a money market product by dint of the term to maturity of repo trades, the nature of the underlying collateral means that repo dealers must be keenly aware of the assets that they 'trade' as well. The assets will be bonds, equity or other collateral of value. This multi-faceted nature of repo is apparent in the way that banks organise their repo trading. In some banks it is part of the money market or Treasury division, while in other banks it will be within the bond trading area. Equity repo is sometimes a back-office activity, as is the longer established stock borrowing desk. However, it is not only commercial and investment banks that engage in repo transactions. Across the world, repo is a well-established investment product, utilised by fund managers, hedge funds, corporate treasuries and local authorities. The practicality and simplicity of repo means that it can be taken up even in capital markets that are still at an 'emerging' stage, and by a wide range of participants. It is traded in virtually every country with a debt capital market.

The use of repo enhances the liquidity of bond and equity markets, which reduces costs for issuers of capital, and allows market makers to hedge positions with greater efficiency. Given its size and importance, it is surprising that repo has such a low profile – for example, there is little discussion of it in the financial press. This reflects the simple and straightforward nature of the instrument. Indeed, the fundamental nature of repo is its simplicity: the sale of securities coupled with an agreement to repurchase them at a future date – in other words, a secured loan of cash. It is this simplicity and flexibility that has allowed repo to be used for a variety of purposes, or to meet a range of requirements.

IMPORTANCE OF REPO

Previous literature highlights the importance of the repo market. In Professor Frank Fabozzi's book *Securities Lending and Repurchase Agreements* (FJF Associates 1997), Kenneth Miller of Goldman Sachs writes:

The global fixed income markets could not be as large as they are today without the parallel existence of a highly liquid, low credit risk vehicle in which participants can borrow cash and securities. The repurchase agreement (repo) is the foundation for the fixed-income markets. Without repo, the development of a liquid derivatives market, notably swaps and financial futures, would not have been possible. (p. 13)

Robert Sloan of Credit Suisse First Boston writing in the same book states:

If one looks at many fixed income desks, it is easy to see that the repo desk is at the hub of the trading floor... the repo desk is the centre of activity... the repo desk functions as the spoke in the wheel for almost all fixed income activities: government [bond] auctions, option pricing, corporate bond financing and customer leverage...
  The repo desk is also organized to fund the firm's inventory. This was the original intent of the repo desk. (p. 248)

So we can see that repo is an important product and a vital part of the financial markets. Most market participants will need to be familiar with it, or at least the concept of it, in order to better understand the nature of their own roles.

There are a number of benefits in using repo, which concurrently have been behind its rapid growth. These include the following:

- bank dealers are able to finance their long bond and equity positions at a lower interest cost if they repo out the assets; equally, they are able to cover 'short' positions;

- there is greater liquidity in specific individual bond issues;
- greater market liquidity lowers the cost of raising funds for capital market borrowers;
- central banks use repo in their open market operations, which assist in the maintenance of overall money market liquidity;
- repo reduces *counterparty risk* in money market borrowing and lending, because of the security offered by the collateral given in the loan;
- investors have an added investment option when placing funds;
- institutional investors and other long-term holders of securities are able to enhance their returns by making their inventories available for repo trading.

There is a close relationship between repo and both the bond and money markets. The use of repo has contributed greatly to the liquidity of government, Eurobond and emerging market bond markets. Although it is a separate and individual market itself, operationally repo is straightforward to handle, in that it generally settles through clearing mechanisms used for bonds. As a money market product, repo reduces the stress placed on the unsecured interbank market, and empirical evidence indicates a reduction in overnight interest-rate volatility.

MARKET PARTICIPANTS

The development and use of repo in each country to an extent dictates the nature and range of market participants. In a mature market, repo counterparties include investors and cash-rich institutions, those seeking to finance asset positions and their intermediaries. Some firms will cross over these broad boundaries and engage all aspects of repo trading. The main market parties are:

- *Financial institutions* – retail and commercial banks, building societies, securities houses and investment banks.
- *Investors* – fund managers, insurance companies and pension funds, investment funds, hedge funds, local authorities and corporate treasuries.
- *Intermediaries* – inter-dealer brokers and money brokers. The main brokers are Cantor Fitzgerald, Prebon Yamane, Garban ICAP, Tullett & Tokyo, and Tradition. Indiviual markets also have other brokers.

Repo is perhaps the most important financial instrument in the world, after the basic cash equity and bond product. An understanding of it is vital for all participants in the financial markets, be they students or practitioners.

THE REPO INSTRUMENT

A repo agreement is a transaction in which, legally, one party sells securities to another, and at the same time and as part of the same transaction commits to repurchase identical securities on a specified date in the future at a specified price. The seller delivers securities and receives cash from the buyer. The cash is supplied at a predetermined interest rate – the *repo rate* – that remains constant during the term of the trade. On maturity the original seller receives back collateral of equivalent type and quality, and returns the cash plus repo interest. One party to the repo requires either the cash or the securities and provides *collateral* to the other party, as well as some form of compensation for the temporary use of the desired asset. Although legal title to the securities is transferred, the seller/ borrower retains both the economic benefits and the market risk of owning them.

Characteristics of repo

There are a number of repo types in operation in different markets. They differ in detail only, and in the motivation behind their use: the economic impact of all of them is essentially identical. The different types are:

- *Classic repo* – the basic form of repo and what is generally understood to be in use when one refers to a 'repo trade'. This is a secured loan conducted under a standard legal agreement, defined as the sale of an asset at a specified price, with an undertaking to repurchase the asset or an equivalent asset at the repo maturity date. A repo is a sale and repurchase, while a buy and subsequent sale is a *reverse repo*.
- *Buy/Sell-back* – economically, identical to a classic repo, and until 1995 (when the transaction was included in the standard repo legal agreement) often not conducted under a legal agreement. A buy/sell was in theory two separate transactions, with the repo interest incorporated into the sell-back price of the asset on maturity, referred to as the *forward price*.

- *Stock loan* or *securities lending* – a transaction motivated by a requirement to borrow a bond or equity, often for the purpose of short-position covering. In a stock loan, a security is lent out for a fixed term or on overnight roll, with collateral, usually in the form of cash, given up in return. The lender of stock pays interest on the collateral during the term of the repo, this interest being known as the *rebate*. A fee is charged by the stock lender for this business.
- *Collateralised loan* – this is a straightforward bank loan, but with collateral given up by the cash borrower.
- *Total return swap* – these days this is classified as a credit derivative, although their use pre-dates that of credit default swaps. A total return swap (*TRS*) has the same economic effect as a repo, and is sometimes called a 'synthetic repo'. It is materially different in that it is carried out under a different legal agreement to that of classic repo, and it is treated differently for capital, tax, accounting and regulatory purposes. We discuss this in Chapter 4.

To begin with we shall consider the operation of *classic* repo, the type prevalent in most markets.

Classic repo

There will be two parties to a repo trade, let us say Bank A (the seller of securities) and Bank B (the buyer of securities). On the trade date the two banks enter into an agreement whereby on a set date, the *value* or *settlement* date, Bank A will sell to Bank B a nominal amount of securities in exchange for cash. The price received for the securities will be linked to the settlement price of the stock on the trade date. The agreement also demands that on the termination date Bank B will sell identical stock back to Bank A at the previously agreed price, and consequently Bank B will have its cash returned with interest at the agreed repo rate.

In essence, a repo agreement is a secured loan (or *collateralised* loan) in which the repo rate reflects the interest charged. The mechanism is illustrated in Figure 1.1.

A *reverse repo* is the mirror image of a repo; that is, purchasing the bond and then selling it back on termination. Of course, every repo is a reverse repo, depending from which party's point of view one is looking at the transaction.

First leg

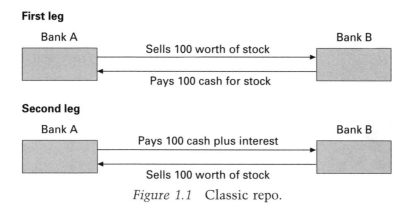

Figure 1.1 Classic repo.

Example 1.1 Classic repo transaction.

To illustrate the basic principle, consider the following. This illustrates a *specific* repo – that is, one in which the collateral supplied is specified as a particular stock as opposed to a *general collateral* (*GC*) trade in which a basket of collateral can be supplied, of any particular issue, as long as it is of the required type and credit quality.

In this example, on 22 December 2005 Bank B agrees to sell £10 million nominal of a United Kingdom gilt, the 5% Treasury 2012, which is trading at a *dirty* price of 104.7079. The agreement will begin on 23 December, the value date. The term of the trade is specified as 1 month or 30 days, but the termination date is 23 January 2006 and not 22 January because the latter is not a business day; hence, the actual term is 31 days. The agreed repo rate for the (effectively collateralised) loan is set at 4.50%, the 1-month repo rate for UK Government stock (see Figure 1.3). On 23 December Bank A receives £10m nominal 5% Treasury 2012 stock, which has a settlement value of £10,570,790 (clean price plus accrued interest).[1]

On 23 January 2006 Bank B receives back the gilt and returns the original cash amount of £10,570,790 along with a repo interest payment of £40,400.69. This is shown in Figure 1.4.

---

[1] The concept of clean and dirty prices, and accrued interest, is covered in Chapter 2 where we look at market background.

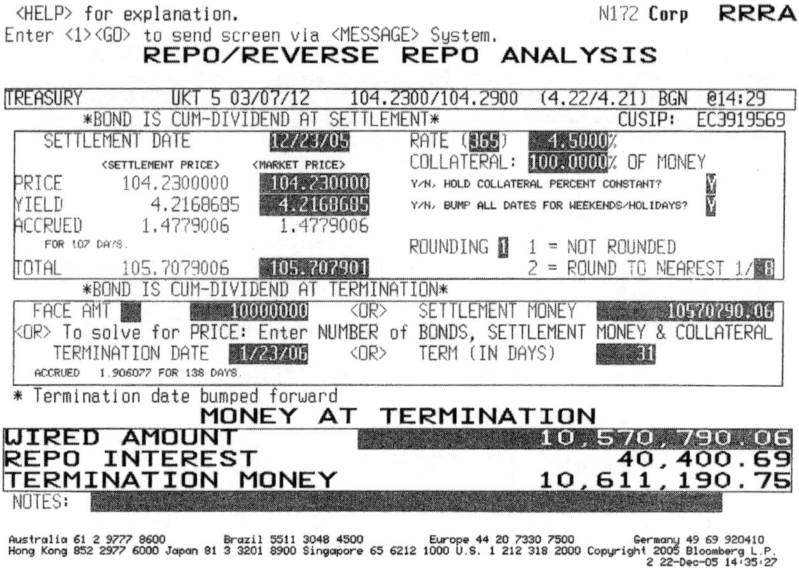

Figure 1.2   RRRA screen as at 22 December 2005, 1-month repo of GBP 10 million nominal 5% Treasury 2012.

© Bloomberg L.P. Used with permission. Visit *www.bloomberg.com*

Figure 1.2 is the Bloomberg page RRRA for this trade, showing the cash flows we describe above. Figure 1.3 is the HBOS repo rates screen for 22 December 2005, showing the 1-month UK repo rate as 4.50%.

The repo interest is based on a 30-day repo rate of 4.50% and a 365-day-count basis. Repo rates are agreed at the time of the trade and are quoted, like all interest rates, on an annualised basis. The repo interest under the agreement equals the cash loaned multiplied by the repo rate, multiplied by the term of the loan as a proportion of the year:

$$10,570,790.06 \times \frac{4.50}{100} \times \frac{32}{365} = £40,400.69$$

The settlement price (dirty price) is used because it is the market value of the bonds on the particular trade date and, hence, indicates the cash value of the gilts. The object is to minimise credit exposure by equating the value of the cash and the collateral.

Page 1 of 1
14:29 GMT
22-Dec-05

	EUR			GBP
	Bid / Offer			Bid / Offer
TN	2.38 / 2.35		1W	4.55 / 4.45
SN	2.38 / 2.35		2W	4.50 / 4.40
SW	2.45 / 2.42		3W	4.50 / 4.40
1MTH	2.34 / 2.31		1M	4.50 / 4.40
2MTH	2.36 / 2.33		2M	4.50 / 4.40
3MTH	2.41 / 2.38		3M	4.48 / 4.38
4MTH	2.46 / 2.43		4M	4.47 / 4.37
5MTH	2.51 / 2.48		5M	4.45 / 4.35
6MTH	2.55 / 2.52		6M	4.43 / 4.33
7MTH	2.59 / 2.56		9M	4.40 / 4.30
8MTH	2.63 / 2.60		1Y	4.38 / 4.28
9MTH	2.67 / 2.64			
10MTH	2.70 / 2.67			
11MTH	2.73 / 2.70			
YR	2.76 / 2.73			

Australia 61 2 9777 8600   Brazil 5511 3048 4500   Europe 44 20 7330 7500   Germany 49 69 920410
Hong Kong 852 2977 6000 Japan 81 3 3201 8900 Singapore 65 6212 1000 U.S. 1 212 318 2000 Copyright 2005 Bloomberg L.P.
3 22-Dec-05 14:35:31

Figure 1.3   HBOS screen for gilt repo rates as at 22 December 2005.
© HBOS plc. © Bloomberg L.P. Used with permission. Visit *www.bloomberg.com*

Note how we have lent the market value of the stock against the collateral – that is, there is no *margin* or *haircut*. A margin is just like the deposit on a house purchase, it protects the cash lender against a fall in value of the collateral. In practice, margin is always taken and can range from 2% to 50% of the collateral value, depending on the perceived risk of the transaction from the cash lender's point of view.

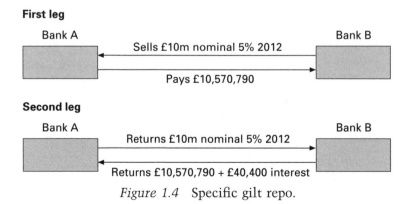

Figure 1.4   Specific gilt repo.

What if the trade is initiated the other way? Imagine a bank has £10 million to invest, and wishes to receive UK gilt securities as collateral. This is the same trade, we just adjust the calculation to determine how much securities we need to pass over. Example 1.2 shows the calculation using the same security, the 5% 2012 gilt, that we looked at above.

Example 1.2   Classic repo: investor's example.

On 22 December 2005, a corporate wishes to invest GBP 10 million against UK Government bonds for 1 month. The collateral is the 5% gilt due in March 2012. The repo rate is agreed at 4.61%. The gilt price is 104.22 clean, which together with 1.4779 accrued interest (107 days) gives a dirty price of 105.6979.

The borrower of cash will need to determine the face value of gilts required at current market price that will equate to GBP 10 million. This is shown below:

$$\frac{105.6979}{100.0000} \times \frac{10,000,000}{X}$$

The nominal value of bonds required (X) is 9,460,925.90. This is rounded to the nearest GBP 1.00 in practice, although gilts can trade in amounts down to GBP 0.01.

The start proceeds are therefore 9,460,925 × 105.6979%, which is in fact GBP 9,999,999.10, although in practice the whole amount will be exchanged. The trade details are summarised below:

Nominal	GBP 9,460,925 of 5% 2012
Clean start price	104.22
Accrued	1.4779
Dirty start price	105.6979
Settlement money	GBP 10,000,000.00
Dirty end price	105.6979
Repo interest	GBP 39,153.42
	[10,000,123 × 4.61% × 31/365]
Termination money	GBP 10,039,153.42

Note that the sale and repurchase prices are the same.

Summary

In a classic repo then, as we have seen, one party sells assets such as bonds to another while simultaneously agreeing to repurchase them on a future date at a specified price. The sale and repurchase prices are the same, although settlement values will differ because on termination of the repo the interest is added on. If a coupon is paid it will be handed over to the seller on the coupon value date. This is known as a *manufactured dividend*. This reflects the fact that, although legal title to the collateral passes to the buyer in a repo, economic costs and benefits of the collateral remain with the seller.

A classic repo transaction is subject to a legal contract signed in advance by both parties. A standard document will suffice – it is not necessary to sign a legal agreement prior to each transaction. The standard legal contract is the Bond Market Association (*BMA*)/ International Capital Markets Association (*ICMA*) Global Master Repurchase Agreement (*GMRA*). This is discussed in Chapter 8.

The sell/buy-back[2]

In addition to classic repo there also exists a *buy/sell* or a *sell/buy-back*. A sell/buy-back is defined as an outright sale of a bond on the value date, and an outright repurchase of that bond for value on a *forward* date. In Figure 1.1, the cash flows, therefore, become a sale of the bond at a *spot* price, followed by repurchase of the bond at the *forward* price. The forward price calculated includes the interest on the repo, and is therefore a different price to the spot price.

Hence, we have a spot sale and forward repurchase of bonds transacted simultaneously. The repo rate is not explicit, but is implied in the forward price. If initial margin is required it is given to the provider of cash (the buyer). Any coupon payments during the term are paid to the seller; however, this is done through incorporation into the forward price, so the seller will not receive it immediately.

---

[2] This is also known as a 'buy/sell-back'. Not surprisingly, they mean the same thing!

Until an annex was incorporated into the standard GMRA, generally sell/buy-backs were not subject to a legal agreement; so, in effect the seller had no legal right to any coupon, and there was no provision for margin calls during the term of the trade (known as 'variation margining'). This made the sell/buy-back a higher risk transaction when compared with classic repo, if the counterparty represented relatively high risk.

Example 1.3 shows a sell/buy-back under the same terms as the classic repo in Example 1.1.

Example 1.3   Sell/Buy-back.

Consider the same terms as those in Example 1.1, but in this case as a buy/sell or sell/buy-back transaction. We require the forward bond price, and this is calculated by converting the termination money. The termination money is simply start cash plus interest on the start cash, at the agreed repo rate:

$$\frac{\text{GBP } 10,617,213.68}{\text{GBP } 10,000,000.00} \times 100 = 106.17214$$

The accrued interest *at the time of termination* is subtracted from this price to obtain a forward clean price:

$$106.17214 - 1.9061[138 \text{ days}] = 104.266$$

The trade details are summarised below, and are also shown at Figure 1.5, which is Bloomberg screen BSR, the sell/buy-back calculation page:

Nominal	GBP 10,000,000.00 of UKT 5% 2012
Clean start price	104.29
Accrued	1.4779
Dirty start price	105.7479
Settlement money	GBP 10,580,790.06
Clean end price	104.26606
Accrued	1.906077
Dirty end price	106.17214
Termination money	GBP 10,617,213.68
	(includes repo interest of GBP 40,423.62)

Note that the sale and repurchase prices are now different.

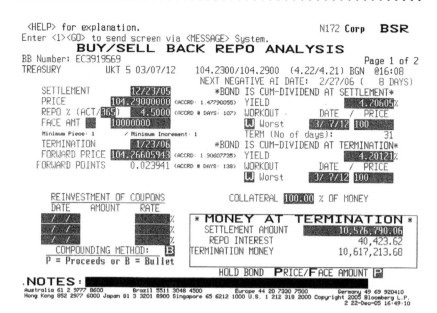

Figure 1.5   BSR screen as at 22 December 2005, 1-month buy/sell-back of GBP 10 millon nominal 5% Treasury 2012.

© Bloomberg L.P. Used with permission. Visit *www.bloomberg.com*

Stock lending

Institutional investors such as pension funds and insurance companies often prefer to enhance the income from their fixed interest portfolios by lending their bonds, for a fee, rather than get involved in repo. A stock loan is a contract committing one party to lend, and the other to borrow, agreed securities for an agreed period. The borrower of stock is required to provide collateral to the lender in the form of cash, other securities or a letter of credit. The origins and history of the stock lending market are different from that of the repo market. The range of counterparties is also different, although of course a large number of counterparties are involved in both markets. Most stock loans are on an 'open' basis, although term loans also occur. Initial margin is given to the lender of the securities.

Example 1.4   Securities lending.

A dealer needs to borrow GBP 10 million nominal of a specific issue, the 5% gilt due March 2012, from 22 December 2005 to

23 January 2006. A pension fund has agreed to lend the stock against collateral, and requires a margin of 102%. The agreed rebate is 4.65%, which is Libor-flat, and the stock loan fee is 10 basis points.

The cash flows for this stock loan are shown below:

Bonds borrowed	GBP 10,000,000.00 of UKT 5% 2012
Clean price	104.29
Accrued	1.4779
Dirty price	105.7679
Market value	GBP 10,000,000.00 × 105.7679%
	= GBP 10,576,790.00
Settlement money	GBP 10,788,325.86
	$[102\% \times 10,576,790.06]^3$
Term	31 days
Rebate rate	4.65%
Rebate interest	GBP 42,606.50
	$[10,788,325.86 \times 4.65\% \times 31/365]$
Termination money	GBP 10,830,932.36
	[GBP 10,788,325.86 + 42,606.50]

The stock loan fee is 10 basis points of the market value of the loan, which for the term involved is GBP 898.30.

Note that initial margin is provided to the lender of the bonds, because the lender requires collateral. The rebate interest, paid to the borrower of the bonds, is at a higher rate than the GC repo rate used in Example 1.1, because it is the (1-month) London Interbank Offered Rate (*Libor*) rate. Libor is higher than the government bond repo rate.

OTHER REPO PRODUCTS

The basic repo product can be dealt in a number of different structures, to suit specific bank customer requirements.

---

[3] Note that this method gives a slightly different answer compared with that of the Bloomberg method, which we discuss in Chapter 3.

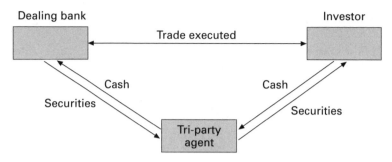

Figure 1.6   Tri-party repo.

Tri-party repo

This is a mechanism (Figure 1.6) that allows dealers maximum control over their inventory, incurs minimal settlement cost to the investor, but gives the investor independent confirmation that their cash is fully collateralised.

Under a tri-party agreement, the dealer delivers collateral to an independent third-party custodian, such as Euroclear or Clearstream, who will place it in a segregated tri-party account.[4] The dealer maintains control over which precise securities are in this account (multiple substitutions are permitted) but the custodian undertakes to confirm each day to the investor that their cash remains fully collateralised by securities of suitable quality. A tri-party agreement needs to be in place with all three parties before trading can commence.

This arrangement reduces the administrative burden for the end-investor, but is not in theory as secure as a conventional delivery-versus-payment structure. Consequently, the yield on the investor's cash (assuming collateral of identical credit quality) should be slightly higher. Tri-party repo is used more when the collateral is non-government bonds, such as Eurobonds, structured finance securities such as asset-backed securities (ABS), and more esoteric assets such as convertible bonds.

---

[4] These are the two international securities clearing systems. Banks such as JPMorgan Chase and Bank of New York also offer tri-party dealing.

Hold in custody repo

This is a sector of the GC market, and exists in the United States only. Consider the case of a cash-rich institution investing in GC as an alternative to deposits or commercial paper. When it comes to the rate of return on their cash, the rules of risk and reward apply. The better the quality of collateral, the lower the yield the institution can expect.

Similarly, the mechanics of settlement may also affect the repo rate. The most secure procedure is to take physical possession of the collateral. However, if the dealer needs one or more substitutions during the term of the trade, the settlement costs involved may make the trade unworkable for one or both parties. Therefore, the dealer may offer to hold the securities in his own custody against the investor's cash. This is known as *hold in custody* (*HIC*) repo (Figure 1.7). The advantage of this trade is that, since securities do not physically move, no settlement charges are incurred. However, this is a risky trade for the investor because they only have the dealer's word that their cash is indeed fully collateralised in the event of default. Thus, this type of trade is sometimes referred to as a 'trust me' repo.

In the US market there have been cases where securities houses having defaulted were found to have pledged the same collateral for multiple HIC repo trades. Investors dealing in HIC repo must ensure:

- they only invest with dealers of good credit quality, since an HIC repo may be perceived as an unsecured transaction;
- the investor receives a higher yield on their cash in order to compensate them for the higher credit risk involved.

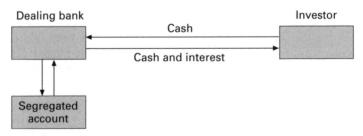

Figure 1.7   HIC repo.

Safe-keeping repo

This is a form of repo whereby the collateral from the repo seller is not delivered to the cash lender but held in 'safe keeping' by the seller. This has advantages in that there is no administration and cost associated with the movement of stock. The risk is that the cash lender must entrust the safe keeping of collateral to the counterparty, and has no means of confirming that the security is indeed segregated, and only being used for one transaction.

Borrow/Loan versus cash

This is similar in almost all respects to a classic repo/reverse repo. A legal agreement between the two parties is necessary, and trades generally settle "delivery versus payment" (*DVP*). The key difference is that under a repo agreement legal title over the collateral changes hands. Under a securities lending agreement this is not necessarily the case. The UK standard securities lending agreement does involve transfer of title, but it is possible to construct a securities lending agreement where legal title does not move. This can be an advantage for customers who may have accounting or tax problems in doing a repo trade. Such institutions will opt to transact a *loan versus cash*. The UK standard lending agreement also covers items such as dividends and voting rights, and is therefore the preferred transaction structure in the equity repo market.

Bonds borrowed/collateral pledged

In this instance the institution lending the bonds does not want or need to receive cash against them, as it is already cash-rich and would only have to re-invest any further cash generated. As such this transaction only occurs with *special collateral*. The dealer borrows the special bonds and pledges securities of similar quality and value (GC). The dealer builds in a fee payable to the lending institution as an incentive to do the trade.

Example 1.5   Bonds borrowed/collateral pledged.

ABC Bank plc wishes to borrow DKK 300 million of the Danish Government bond 8% 2001. ABC owns the Danish Government bond 7% 2007. ABC is prepared to pay a customer a 40-bps fee in order to borrow the 8% 2001 for 1 month.

The market price of the 8% 2001 (including accrued interest) is 112.70. The total value of DKK 300 million nominal is therefore DKK 338,100,000.

The market price of the 7% 2007 (including accrued interest) is 102.55.

In order to fully collateralise the customer, ABC needs to pledge 338,100,000/1.0255 which is 329,692,832.76, which rounded to the nearest DKK 1 million becomes DKK 330 million nominal of the 7% 2007.

In a bonds borrowed/collateral pledged trade, both securities are delivered free of payment and ABC Bank plc would pay the customer a 40-basis points borrowing fee upon termination. In our example the fee payable would be:

$$338,100,000 \times \frac{31}{360} \times \frac{0.4}{100} = \text{DKK } 112,700$$

Cross-currency repo

All of the examples discussed so far have used cash and securities denominated in the same currency; for example, Bunds trading versus euros cash, and so on. However, there is no requirement to limit oneself to single-currency transactions.

It is possible to trade, say, UK gilts versus US dollar cash (or any other currency), or pledge Spanish Government bonds against borrowing Japanese Government bonds. Note that:

- there may be significant daylight credit exposure on the transaction if securities cannot settle versus payment;
- the transaction must be covered by the appropriate legal documentation;
- fluctuating foreign exchange rates mean that it is likely that the transaction will need to be marked-to-market frequently in order to ensure that cash or securities remain fully collateralised.

Exotic repo structures

Four-party repo

A four-party repo is similar to a tri-party repo except that there are
two custodians or agents instead of one. A second sub-custodian is
added to the trade, who is in practice holding and administering the
cash and collateral. This arrangement is usually entered into for legal
or operational restrictions that state that a certain custodian or legal
jurisdiction is required; the second custodian is appointed due to
restrictions that prevent the primary custodian from acting in the
trade

Floating-rate repo

As with an unsecured loan, repo can be transacted with a floating
interest rate, reset at specified intervals and at a set spread over or
under the reference index. Floating-rate repo is often entered into
where the collateral asset also has a floating rate, with the reset date
set to match the coupon frequency of the asset.

Flex repo

A flexible or 'flex' repo is one in which the nominal amount can be
adjusted during the term of the repo. For example, a corporate may
place funds in repo for a 1-year term at a 3-month floating rate. If it
requires part of its cash before maturity, it can draw down from the
repo. The repo nominal is adjusted downwards to reflect this. Flex
repo is common in the US market where the collateral is mortgage-
backed securities (MBS), or other securities that have prepayment
features. As the nominal amount of the collateral is paid down, the
repo nominal is adjusted to match this. Flex repo using MBS or ABS
securities is sometimes called 'structured repo'.

Collateral swap

A collateral swap is in effect a repo, as it is a funding trade, and is
common where equity collateral is used. A market maker will accept
stock in the swap and exchange other securities as collateral. Depending on the credit quality of each type of collateral, the market
maker can repo out higher quality collateral to pay a lower repo rate.

SELECTED REFERENCES

Choudhry, M. (2002). *The REPO Handbook*. Butterworth-Heinemann.
Fabozzi, F. (1997). *Securities Lending and Repurchase Agreements*. FJF
   Associates.

Chapter

2

....

MARKET BACKGROUND

Repo is organised as part of the money markets, because the term of repo trades falls within 1 year. As essential background we need to be familiar with money market products. In addition, as bonds are the most common form of repo collateral, we need to be very familiar with bond instruments as well. This chapter provides the necessary detail, including a discussion on discounting and present value. Readers already familiar with money market and bond market instruments can go straight to Chapter 3.

DISCOUNTING AND PRESENT VALUE

The principles of compound interest have for some time now been used to illustrate that £1 received today is not the same as £1 received at a point in the future. Faced with a choice between £1 today or £1 in 1 year's time we would not be indifferent, given a rate of interest of, say, 10% per annum. Our choice would be between £1 today and £1 plus 10p a year from now – the interest on £1 for 1 year at 10% per annum. The further one goes into the future, the greater will be requirement to be compensated for interest foregone, because of the effect of compounding.

Compounding

In compounding we seek to find a *future value* given a *present value*, a *time period* and an *interest rate*. If £100 is invested today (at time t_0) at 10%, then 1 year later (t_1) the investor will have £100 × (1 + 0.10) = £110. If he leaves the capital and interest for another year he will have at the end of year 2 (t_2):

$$£110 \times (1 + 0.10) = £100 \times (1 + 0.10) \times (1 + 0.10)$$

$$= £100 \times (1 + 0.10)^2$$

$$= £121$$

The outcome of the process of compounding is the *future value* of the initial amount. Therefore we can use the following expression:

$$FV = PV(1 + r)^n \qquad (2.1)$$

where FV = Future value;
          PV = Initial outlay or *present value*;
          r = Periodic rate of interest (expressed as decimal);
          n = Number of periods for which the sum is invested.

Formula (2.1) assumes annual compounding. Where semi-annual or quarterly compounding takes place, the equation is modified as shown in equation (2.3).

Discounting

The relationship established above can be reversed to find the *present value* (*PV*) of a known future sum. The formula then becomes:

$$PV = \frac{FV}{(1 + r)^n} \qquad (2.2)$$

Example 2.1   Present value.

Angela requires £1,000 in 3 years' time, and can invest at 9%. How much does she need to invest now?

To solve this she requires the *PV* of £1,000 received in 3 years' time:

$$PV = \frac{1,000}{(1 + 0.09)^3}$$

$$= \frac{1,000}{1.295} = £772.20$$

So, she needs to invest £773 now to ensure her target return is met.

Essentially, in Example 2.1 the prospective future value of £1,000 was multiplied by $1/(1 + 0.09)^3$, which is called the *discount factor*, and which had to be calculated. Tables of these factors already exist, called *discount tables* or *present value tables*, showing the *PV* of £1 received after *n* years at *r* rate of interest.

Compounding more than once a year

When interest is compounded more than once a year, the formula for calculating present values must be modified:

$$PV = \frac{C_n}{\left(1 + \dfrac{r}{m}\right)^{mn}} \qquad (2.3)$$

where C_n = Cash flow at the end of year *n*;
                 m = Number of times a year interest is compounded;
                        and
                 r = Rate of interest as before.

Therefore the present value of £100 to be received at the end of Year 3, at a rate of interest rate of 10% compounded quarterly, is:

$$PV = \frac{100}{\left(1 + \frac{0.10}{4}\right)^{(4)(3)}}$$

$$= £74.36$$

Internal rate of return

The internal rate of return or yield for an investment is the discount rate that equates the present value of the expected cash flows – the *net present value* (*NPV*) – to 0. Mathematically, it is represented by that rate r such that:

$$\sum_{t=1}^{n} \left[\frac{C_t}{(1+r)^t}\right] = 0 \qquad (2.4)$$

where C_t = Cash flow for the period t;
          n = Last period in which a cash flow is expected; and
          $\sum$ = Sum of discounted cash flows at the end of periods 0 through n.

If the initial cash flow occurs at time 0, Equation (2.4) can be expressed as:

$$C_0 = \frac{C_1}{(1+r)} + \frac{C_2}{(1+r)^2} + \cdots + \frac{C_n}{(1+r)^n} \qquad (2.5)$$

Thus, r is the rate that discounts the stream of future cash flows (C_1 through C_n) to equal the initial outlay at time $0 - C_0$. We must therefore assume that the cash flows received subsequently are reinvested to realise the same rate of return as r. This is exactly the same assumption and theory used to construct the yield to maturity equation; in fact, they are measuring the same thing. Solving for the internal rate of return r cannot be found analytically and has to be found through numerical iteration, or using a computer or programmable calculator.

MONEY MARKET INSTRUMENTS

Money market securities are securities with maturities of less than 1 year. Debt market securities with maturities in excess of 1 year are capital market securities. There are two main classes of money market securities: those quoted on a *yield* basis and those quoted on a *discount* basis. Settlement can be for value today (generally, only when traded in the morning), tomorrow or *spot* (2 days' forward).

Securities quoted on a yield basis

Money market deposits

Money market deposits are fixed-interest term deposits of up to 1 year with banks and securities houses. They are not negotiable so cannot be liquidated before maturity. The interest rate on the deposit is fixed for the term and related to the London Interbank Offered Rate (*LIBOR*) of the same term. Interest and capital are paid on maturity.

Certificates of deposit

Certificates of deposit (CDs) are receipts from banks for deposits that have been placed with them. The deposits themselves carry a fixed rate of interest related to LIBOR and have a fixed term to maturity, so cannot be withdrawn before maturity. However, the certificates themselves can be traded in a secondary market – that is, they are negotiable. CDs are therefore very similar to negotiable money market deposits, although the yields are about 0.25% below the equivalent deposit rates because of the added benefit of liquidity. Most CDs issued are of between 1 and 3 months' maturity, although they do trade in maturities of 1 to 5 years. Interest is paid on maturity except for CDs lasting longer than 1 year, where interest is paid annually.

If the current market price of the CD including accrued interest is P and the current yield is r, the yield can be calculated given the price using:

$$r = \left\{ \frac{M}{P} \times \left[1 + d \left(\frac{N_{im}}{365} \right) \right] - 1 \right\} \times \left(\frac{365}{N_{sm}} \right) \tag{2.6}$$

or the price given the yield using:

$$P = M \times \left[1 + d \left(\frac{N_{im}}{365} \right) \right] \Big/ \left[1 + r \left(\frac{N_{sm}}{365} \right) \right]$$

$$= F \Big/ \left[1 + r \left(\frac{N_{sm}}{365} \right) \right] \tag{2.7}$$

where M = Face value of the CD;
           F = Maturity value of the CD;
           N_{im} = Number of days between issue and maturity;
           N_{sm} = Number of days between settlement and maturity;
           N_{is} = Number of days between issue and settlement.

Note that 365 is used in the equations because the UK markets
assume a 365-day year for money market calculations; the US and
euro money markets assume a 360-day year.

Securities quoted on a discount basis

Treasury bills, bills of exchange, banker's acceptances and commercial paper are the most important examples of money market
securities that are quoted on a discount basis – that is, they are sold
on the basis of a discount to par.

- *Treasury bills* – these are short-term government IOUs of
  3 months' duration. If a bill is issued on 10 January it will
  mature on 10 April. On maturity the holder receives the par value
  of the bill by presenting it to the central bank. In the UK most
  such bills are denominated in sterling but issues are also made in
  euros.
- *Bills of exchange* – these are also known as *trade bills* or *commercial bills*. They are similar to Treasury bills but are issued by
  private companies against the sale of goods. They are used to
  finance trade in the short term.
- *Banker's acceptances* – these are written promises issued by
  borrowers to banks to repay borrowed funds. The lending bank
  lends funds and in return accepts the banker's acceptance. The
  acceptance is negotiable and can be sold in a secondary market.
  The investor who buys the acceptance can collect the loan on the
  day that repayment is due. If the borrower defaults, the investor
  has legal recourse to the bank that made the first acceptance.
- *Commercial paper (CP)* – this refers to unsecured promissory
  notes issued by large corporates with maturities of between 1 day
  and 1 year. As the notes are not backed by any collateral they rely
  on the credit rating of the issuing corporation. Therefore, only
  sufficiently large and creditworthy corporates can access this
  market.

All these securities are sold at a discount-to-par value. On maturity
the investor receives the par value. Explicit interest is not paid on

discount instruments, rather interest is reflected implicitly in the difference between the discounted issue price and the par value received at maturity. If we know the yield on these securities, then we can calculate their price at issue by using the simple present value formula, as shown in Equation (2.8):

$$P = M \Big/ \left[1 + r\left(\frac{N_{sm}}{365}\right)\right] \qquad (2.8)$$

This can be illustrated using a Treasury bill. For example, a 91-day £100 Treasury bill issued with a yield of 10.26% would have an issue price of:

$$P = £100 \Big/ \left[1 + 0.1026\left(\frac{91}{365}\right)\right]$$

$$= £97.51$$

Market convention dictates that Treasury bills are not quoted on the basis of a yield, rather they are quoted on the basis of a *discount rate*; the issue price is therefore determined as the difference between the face value and the discount.

The price paid for a bill quoted at a discount rate of d is:

$$P = 100 \times \left[1 - \frac{d \times \left(\frac{N_{sm}}{365}\right)}{100}\right] \qquad (2.9)$$

Money market formulae

A 'quick and dirty' yield formula for money market instruments is:

$$r = \left[\left(\frac{FV}{PV}\right) - 1\right] \times \frac{\text{Day base}}{\text{Days}} \qquad (2.10)$$

The concepts of future value (FV) and present value (PV) were considered on pp. 22–23.

The discount rate $D\%$ for T-Bills is calculated by:

$$D\% = (1 - \text{Price}) \times \frac{365}{\text{Tenor (days)}} \qquad (2.11)$$

Example 2.2   LIBOR.

The term LIBOR or Libor (as already stated) comes from London Interbank Offered Rate and is the interest rate at which one London bank offers funds to another London bank of acceptable credit quality in the form of a cash deposit. The rate is 'fixed' by the British Bankers Association (*BBA*) at 11 : 00 hours every business day morning (in practice, the fix is usually about 20–30 minutes later) by taking the average of the rates supplied by member banks. The term LIBID or Libid is the bank's 'bid' rate – that is, the rate at which it pays for funds in the London market. The quote spread for a selected maturity is therefore the difference between Libor and Libid. The convention in London is to quote the two rates as Libor–Libid, thus matching the yield convention for other instruments. In some other markets the quote convention is reversed. EURIBOR or Euribor is the interbank rate offered for euros as reported by the European Central Bank, fixed in Brussels.

Figure 2.1 shows the Libor fixing page from page BBAM on Bloomberg, with the rate fix for 22 December 2005.

200<GO>to view this page in Launchpad   N1217a **Govt**   **BBAM**

BRITISH BANKERS'
ASSOCIATION   Page 1 of 4

12/23 08:25 GMT [BRITISH BANKERS ASSOCIATION LIBOR RATES]					3750
[22/12/05] RATES AT 11:00 LONDON TIME 22/12/2005. 23/12 03:03 GMT					
CCY	USD	GBP	CAD	EUR	JPY	EUR 365
O/N	4.29500	4.80500	3.22833	2.42750	SN0.04063	2.46122
1WK	4.44875	4.69375	3.26333	2.47888	0.04188	2.51128
2WK	4.38250	4.68625	3.27667	2.44563	0.04188	2.47960
1MO	4.37875	4.65313	3.30167	2.42950	0.04938	2.46324
2MO	4.46813	4.64625	3.37583	2.44163	0.05750	2.47554
3MO	4.51938	4.63938	3.45333	2.48800	0.06750	2.52256
4MO	4.58000	4.62375	3.55167	2.54738	0.07000	2.58276
5MO	4.64225	4.61313	3.64000	2.59525	0.07500	2.63130
6MO	4.71000	4.60000	3.73333	2.64175	0.08063	2.67844
7MO	4.74538	4.59375	3.79000	2.68525	0.08625	2.72255
8MO	4.77900	4.58688	3.84667	2.72063	0.08875	2.75842
9MO	4.81125	4.58375	3.90833	2.75875	0.09313	2.79707
10MO	4.83475	4.58688	3.94333	2.79388	0.10125	2.83268
11MO	4.85650	4.59063	3.97500	2.82388	0.10750	2.86310
12MO	4.88000	4.59625	4.01167	2.85400	0.11688	2.89364

Australia 61 2 9777 8600   Brazil 5511 3048 4500   Europe 44 20 7330 7500   Germany 49 69 920410
Hong Kong 852 2977 6000 Japan 81 3 3201 8900 Singapore 65 6212 1000 U.S. 1 212 318 2000 Copyright 2005 Bloomberg L.P.
                                                                          2 23-Dec-05 8:25:28

Figure 2.1   Bloomberg screen BBAM1, Libor fixing for 22 December 2005.

© Bloomberg L.P. Used with permission. Visit *www.bloomberg.com*

200<GO>to view this page in Launchpad N121 a **Govt** **EBF**

EUROPEAN BANKING
FEDERATION   Page 1 of 1

```
12/23    08:25 GMT    [    EURIBOR FBE/ACI    ]                    240
  EURIBOR RATES ACT/360 AT 11H00 BRUSSELS TIME 22/12/2005    23/12 03:03 GMT
                                  ACT/ 360
                           1WK    2.469    [FIXED]
                           2WK    2.436    VALUE DATE 27/12/05
                           3WK    2.429    [EURIBOR NOTE ON PAGE 47893]
                           1MO    2.426
                           2MO    2.443
                           3MO    2.494
                           4MO    2.549
                           5MO    2.597    [WARNING] EITHER EURIBOR FBE,
                           6MO    2.642    NOR EURIBOR ACI, NOR THE EURIBO
                           7MO    2.682    PANEL BANKS, NOR THE EURIBOR
                           8MO    2.719    STEERING COMMITTEE, NOR REUTERS
                           9MO    2.754    CAN BE HELD LIABLE FOR ANY
[HISTORY] THIS CAN BE     10MO    2.791    IRREGULARITY OR INACCURACY OF
DOWNLOADED FROM THE       11MO    2.821    THE EURIBOR RATE.
WEBSITE WWW.EURIBOR.ORG   12MO    2.852    (FOR DETAILS SEE PAGE 47896)

Australia 61 2 9777 8600      Brazil 5511 3048 4500    Europe 44 20 7330 7500      Germany 49 69 920410
Hong Kong 852 2977 6000 Japan 81 3 3201 8900 Singapore 65 6212 1000 U.S. 1 212 318 2000 Copyright 2005 Bloomberg L.P.
                                                                      2 23-Dec-05  8:25:40
```

Figure 2.2   Bloomberg screen EBF, Euribor fixing for 22 December 2005.

© Bloomberg L.P. Used with permission. Visit *www.bloomberg.com*

Example 2.3   EURIBOR.

The official euro fixing is known as Euribor, which is set in Brussels at 11:00 hours local time on each euro business day. This should not be confused with the euro Libor fixing. The fixing operates in the same way as Libor, with a panel of Euribor banks contributing their rates each morning. The average rate of all contributions is taken as the fix.

Figure 2.2 shows the Euribor fixing page from the European Banking Federation for 22 December 2005.

OVERVIEW OF BOND MARKET INSTRUMENTS

Bonds are debt capital market securities and, therefore, have maturities longer than 1 year. This differentiates them from money market securities. Bonds also have more intricate cash flow patterns than money market securities, which usually have just one cash flow at maturity. This makes bonds more difficult to price than money market instruments, and their prices more responsive to changes in the general level of interest rates.

Definition of a bond

There are a large variety of bonds. The most common type is the *conventional* (or *plain vanilla* or *bullet*) bond. This is a bond paying a regular (annual or semi-annual) fixed-interest payment or *coupon* over a fixed period to maturity or *redemption*, with the return of principal (the par or nominal value of the bond) on the maturity date. All other bonds are variations on this.

Types of issuer

A key feature of a bond is the nature of the issuer. There are four issuers of bonds: governments and their agencies, local governments (or municipal authorities), supranational bodies, and corporates. Within the municipal and corporate markets there are a wide range of issuers, each with varying abilities to satisfy their contractual obligations to the holders of their paper.

Term to maturity

The *term to maturity* of a bond is the number of years over which the issuer has promised to meet the conditions of the obligation. The *maturity* of a bond refers to the date that the debt will cease to exist, at which time the issuer will redeem the bond by paying the principal. The practice in the bond market is to refer to the 'term to maturity' of a bond as simply its 'maturity' or 'term'. Some bonds contain provisions that allow either the issuer or the bondholder to alter a bond's term.

The term to maturity of a bond impacts on its characteristics. First, it indicates the time period over which the bondholder can expect to receive coupon payments and the number of years before the principal is paid back. Second, it influences the yield of a bond. Finally, the price of a bond will fluctuate over its life as yields in the market change. The volatility of a bond's price is dependent on its maturity. All else being equal, the longer the maturity of a bond, the greater the price volatility resulting from a change in market yields.

Principal and coupon rate

The *principal* of a bond is the amount that the issuer agrees to repay the bondholder on maturity. This amount is also referred to as the *redemption value, maturity value, par value* or *face value*.

The coupon rate, or *nominal rate*, is the interest rate that the issuer agrees to pay each year during the life of the bond. The annual amount of interest payment made to bondholders is the *coupon*. The cash amount of the coupon is the coupon rate multiplied by the principal of the bond. For example, a bond with a coupon rate of 8% and a principal of £1,000 will pay annual interest of £80. In the United Kingdom the usual practice is for the issuer to pay the coupon in two semi-annual instalments.

All bonds make periodic coupon payments, except for one type that makes none. These bonds are known as *zero-coupon bonds*. Such bonds are issued at a discount and redeemed at par. The holder of a zero-coupon bond realises interest by buying the bond at this discounted value, below its principal value. Interest is therefore paid on maturity, with the exact amount being the difference between the principal value and the discounted value paid on purchase.

Floating rate bonds (FRNs) also exist. With these bonds coupon rates are reset periodically according to a predetermined benchmark, such as 3-month or 6-month LIBOR. For this reason FRNs typically trade more as money market instruments than conventional bonds.

Fair pricing of bonds and bond yield

A vanilla bond pays a fixed rate of interest (coupon) annually or semi-annually, or very rarely quarterly. The *fair price* of such a bond is given by the discounted present value of the total cash flow stream, using a market-determined discount rate.

Yield to maturity (*YTM*) is the most frequently used measure of return from holding a bond. The YTM is equivalent to the *internal rate of return* on the bond, the rate that equates the value of the discounted cash flows on the bond to its current price. The YTM equation for a bond paying semi-annual coupons is shown as Equation (2.12):

$$P = \sum_{t=1}^{2T} \frac{C/2}{\left(1+\frac{1}{2}r\right)^t} + \frac{M}{\left(1+\frac{1}{2}r\right)^{2T}} \qquad (2.12)$$

where P = Fair price of bond;
                 C = Coupon;
                 M = Redemption payment (par);
                 T = Number of years to maturity;
                 r = Required rate of return on the bond

The solution to this equation cannot be found analytically and has to be solved through iteration – that is, by estimating the yield from two trial values for r, then solving by using the formula for linear interpolation.

While YTM is the most commonly used measure of yield, it has one major disadvantage. The effect of this means that in practice the measure itself will not equal the actual return from holding the bond, even if it is held to maturity. The disadvantage is that implicit in the calculation of the YTM is the assumption that each coupon payment as it becomes due is re-invested at the rate r. This is clearly unlikely, due to fluctuations in interest rates over time and as the bond approaches maturity. That said, the market standard is to quote bond returns as YTMs, bearing the key assumptions behind the calculation in mind.

Yield conventions

Each bond market has its own yield quotation, sometimes referred to as the 'street' or 'consortium' yield. The yield convention is based on the frequency of coupon payment. For example, UK gilts are quoted with semi-annual yields while German Bunds are quoted with annual yields. In order to compare bond yields, they need to be quoted at an *effective* annual rate. This requires all yields that are not quoted as annualised yields to be converted.

To convert between annually and semi-annually quoted yields we can use:

$$\left.\begin{array}{c} r_a = \left[\left(1+\dfrac{1}{2}r_s\right)^2 - 1\right] \\[2ex] r_s = \left[(1+r_a)^{1/2} - 1\right] \times 2 \end{array}\right\} \qquad (2.13)$$

where r_a and r_s represent the annual and semi-annual yield quotations, respectively.

The yield curve

The relationship between a particular yield measure and a bond's maturity is called the *yield curve* or *term structure of interest rates.* To construct a yield curve correctly, only bonds from the same class should be included; for example, bonds with the same credit risk class or with the same degree of liquidity. Therefore, one would not construct a yield curve of, say, both government bonds and corporate bonds. The three yield curves most frequently encountered are the YTM curve, par yield curve and spot yield curve:

- *YTM yield curve* – the most common yield curve is that constructed from the measure for the YTM, or *gross redemption yield*. An example is shown at Figure 2.3.
- *Par yield curve* – this is a plot of the YTM against term to maturity for bonds priced at par. The par yield is therefore equal to the coupon rate for bonds priced at or near par. The curve is used to determine the required coupon on a new bonds that is to be issued at par.

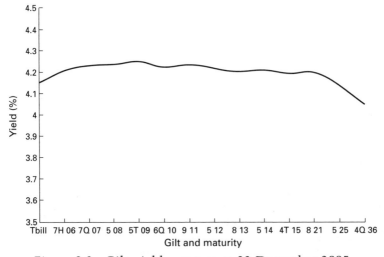

Figure 2.3   Gilt yield curve as at 22 December 2005.

Rates source: Bloomberg.

- *Spot (or zero-coupon) yield curve* – this is a plot of spot yields against term to maturity. Spot rates are also called 'zero-coupon' rates.

Theories of the yield curve

There are several explanations of why yield curves assume particular shapes. The *expectations hypothesis* argues that the long-term interest rate is a geometric average of expected future short-term rates. (This theory is also used to derive forward rates.) A rising yield curve is explained by investors expecting short-term interest rates to rise; a falling yield curve is explained by investors expecting short-term rates to be lower in the future. The main function of these expectations is the expected rate of *inflation*. If investors are expecting inflationary pressures in the future, the yield curve will be *positive* (rising), while if they are expecting disinflationary pressures the yield curve will be *negative* or falling.

The *liquidity preference* theory seeks to explain a positive-sloping yield curve as resulting from investors' preferences to stay liquid. Since borrowers prefer to borrow long-term and lenders prefer to lend short-term, investors have to be compensated by a liquidity premium to forego liquidity over longer maturities, and this premium increases with term to maturity.

The *segmentation* or *preferred habitat* theory argues that the bond market is segmented by maturity range and that there are no spill-over effects between each market segment. The yield curve is therefore determined by supply and demand conditions in each market segment – for example, demand at the short end by banks and building societies and demand at the long end by insurance companies and pension funds. This would explain 'humped' yield curve shapes.

Bond price/yield relationship

The bond price equation has illustrated the relationship between a bond's price and discount rate (the yield measure). The percentage increase in price when yields decline is greater than the percentage decrease when yields rise. This is due to the convex relationship, when plotted on a graph, between price and yield.

The sensitivity of a bond to changes in interest rate is measured by *duration* and *modified duration*. Duration is the weighted average maturity of a bond, using the discounted cash flows of the bond as weights. For a background on duration and modified duration, see Appendix A.

ACCRUED INTEREST

Virtually all bond issuers pay coupon interest once or twice a year, although most floating-rate bonds pay quarterly or monthly coupon. An investor selling a bond between two coupon payments will receive from the purchaser the interest that has accrued on the bond since the last coupon payment. To the bond's 'clean' market price is added the accrued interest, resulting in the 'dirty' price, or price of the bond plus accrued interest, which reflects the actual cash proceeds of the trade. Traders deal in clean prices; the back office deals with the accrued interest and total consideration.

Accrual conventions

The accrued interest calculation for a bond is dependent on the day-count basis specified for the bond in question. There are four types:

act/365   Accrued = Coupon × Days/365
act/360   Accrued = Coupon × Days/360
act/act   Accrued = Coupon × Days/actual number of days in the interest period
30/360   Accrued = Coupon × '360 days'/360 (assumes 30 days in each month)

The day-count basis in selected countries is:

France   act/act
Germany   act/act
Italy   act/act
UK   act/act
Australia   act/360
Japan   act/365
USA   act/act
South Africa act/365

For further detail and worked examples see Choudhry (2004b).

SELECTED BIBLIOGRAPHY

Choudhry, M. (2004a). *Analysing and Interpreting the Yield Curve.* John Wiley & Sons.

Choudhry, M. (2004b). *Fixed Income Markets: Instruments, Applications, Mathematics.* John Wiley & Sons.

Choudhry, M. (2005). *The Money Markets Handbook.* John Wiley & Sons.

Chapter
3

....

THE MECHANICS OF REPO

In this chapter we talk further on the use of repo, and the mechanics of its daily operation. Repo is in essence a funding tool; it enables a market participant to obtain cash in order to fund positions. Alternatively, it is a means by which banks and other financial institutions can obtain specific securities. In this chapter we discuss further the background to and motivation behind repo trades. We also consider risk management issues associated with dealing in repo.

USES AND ECONOMIC FUNCTIONS

The repo mechanism allows for compensation for use of a desired asset. If cash is the desired asset, the compensation for its use is simply the repo rate of interest paid on it. If bonds are the desired asset, the buyer of stock (lender of cash) compensates the seller (borrower) by accepting a below-market repo rate of interest on cash lent out. Otherwise, the repo is a standard money market transaction, with the repo rate a function of the credit quality of the cash borrower, quality of collateral used and the term of the loan.

Funding positions

In the normal course of business a bond trader or market maker will need to finance his positions. Figure 3.1 illustrates the basic principle for a bond trader who has purchased bonds. Figure 3.2 shows the interaction of the repo desk in a bond financing trade.

To finance the position the bond trader can borrow money unsecured in the interbank market, assuming that he has a credit line in this market. However, a collateralised loan will invariably be offered to him at a lower rate, and counterparties are more likely to have a credit line for the bond trader if the loan is secured.

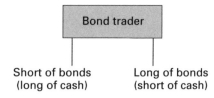

Figure 3.1   Financing bond positions.

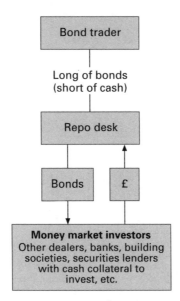

Figure 3.2   Repo desk funding of bond position.

Repo as a financing transaction

Cash-rich money market investors finance bond traders by lending out cash in a repo. They receive *general collateral (GC)* in return for their cash, which is any bond of the required credit quality. Legally, this is a sale and repurchase of bonds; economically, it is a secured loan of cash. The cash investor receives the repo rate of interest for making the loan.

The advantages of a repo transaction for the cash investor are:

- it is a secured investment;
- the returns are competitive with bank deposits and occasionally higher;
- this is a diversification from bank risk.

Covering short positions

A bond trader will enter into a *reverse repo* when he requires a specific issue to deliver into a short sale. In this case the trader is effectively borrowing bonds and putting up cash as collateral. The bond trader receives the repo rate on his cash.

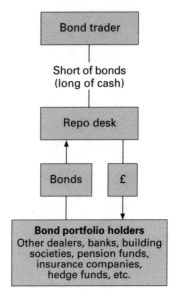

Figure 3.3   Reverse repo trade.

The position is shown in Figure 3.3.

In this transaction the bond lender's compensation is the difference between the repo rate paid on the dealer's cash and the market rate at which he can re-invest the cash. If the bond is particularly sought after – that is, it is *special* – the repo rate may be significantly below the GC rate. Special status in a bond will push the repo rate downwards. Zero rates and even negative rates are possible when dealing in specials.

Supply and demand

The repo rate will reflect supply and demand in the market. In a financing transaction, the dealer is paying the repo rate on the investor's cash. The GC rate tends to trade below the London Interbank Offered Rate (*LIBOR*), and also below the LIBID rate, reflecting its status as a secured loan backed with high-quality collateral (government bonds). In a positioning transaction, the dealer receives the repo rate on his cash. If the bond being borrowed (for this is, in effect, what is happening) is special, the repo rate receivable will be lower to reflect the demand for the bond.

Yield enhancement

Active players in repo and interbank markets can enhance yield by lending bonds at the GC rate and then re-investing the cash at a higher rate. This would of course introduce an element of credit risk. A market counterparty could also borrow bonds in the stock lending market, on-lend these bonds via repo and invest the cash proceeds in, say, CDs. Where the collateral is government bonds, the institution will usually be receiving a higher rate on the CD than the repo rate it is paying in the repo. The use of repo for arbitrage and basis trading will be considered in a later section.

MARGIN

We introduced the concept of margin in Chapter 1. This is where the market value of collateral is adjusted so that it is greater than the amount of cash being lent. This is to protect the cash lender from a drop in value of the collateral. The size of the margin, also called a *haircut*, is a function of the quality of the collateral, the volatility of the market and the credit quality of the counterparty. Margin is taken at the start of the trade and also, if needed, during the term of the trade. The latter is known as *variation* margin.

Initial margin

The start proceeds of a repo can be less than the market value of the collateral by an agreed amount or percentage, the margin. The initial margin protects the buyer against:

- a sudden fall in the market value of the collateral;
- illiquidity of collateral;
- other sources of volatility of value (e.g., approaching maturity);
- counterparty risk.

The margin level of repo varies from 0%–2% for collateral such as UK gilts to 5%–10% for cross-currency and equity repo to 10%–35% for emerging market debt repo. In both classic repo and sell/buy-back, any initial margin is given to the supplier of cash in the transaction. This remains the case in specific issue transactions. For initial margin the market value of the bond collateral is reduced (or given a 'haircut', hence the name) by the percentage of the initial margin and the nominal value determined from this reduced amount.

There are two methods for calculating the margin; for example, for a 2% margin this could be one of the following:

- the dirty price of the bonds $\times 0.98$;
- the dirty price of the bonds/1.02.

Note that the Bloomberg system uses the second method for its calculations. It is important for counterparties to be clear on which method is being used because they do not give the same answer.

So, an initial margin of, say, 2% can be either 2% of the value of the collateral or 2% of the value of the cash. The first example would be:

$$\text{Collateral value} \times (1.00 - 0.02) = 98\%$$

$$\text{Nominal value} \times \text{Dirty price} \times (1.00 - 0.02) = 98\%$$

The second case is calculated as:

$$\frac{\text{Collateral value}}{(1.00 + 0.02)} = 98.039\%$$

$$\text{Nominal} \times \frac{\text{Dirty price}}{(1.00 + 0.02)} = 98.039\%$$

The Bond Market Association (BMA)/International Capital Markets Association ($ICMA$) Global Master Repurchase Agreement ($GMRA$) defines a 'margin ratio' as:

$$\frac{\text{Collateral value}}{\text{Cash}} = 102\%$$

The size of margin required in any particular transaction is a function of the following:

- the credit quality of the counterparty supplying the collateral;
- the term of the repo;
- the duration (price volatility) of the collateral;
- the existence or absence of a legal agreement.

However, in the final analysis, margin is required to guard against market risk, the risk that the value of collateral will drop during the course of the repo. Therefore, the margin call must reflect the risks prevalent in the market at the time; extremely volatile market conditions may call for large increases in initial margin.

Variation margin

The market value of the collateral is maintained through the use of *variation margin*. So, if the market value of the collateral falls, the buyer calls for extra cash or collateral. If the market value of the collateral rises, the seller calls for extra cash or collateral. In order to reduce the administrative burden, margin calls can be limited to changes in the market value of the collateral in excess of an agreed amount or percentage, which is called a *margin maintenance limit*. An example of variation margin being applied during the term of a trade is given at Example 3.1.

The standard market documentation that exists for the three repo structures covered so far (in addition to tri-party repo) include clauses that allow parties to a transaction to call for variation margin during the term of a repo. This can be in the form of extra collateral, if the value of the collateral has dropped in relation to the asset exchanged, or a return of collateral, if the value has risen. Both parties have an interest in making and meeting margin calls, although there is no obligation unless the deal is conducted under the standard GMRA. The level at which variation margin is triggered is often agreed beforehand in the legal agreement put in place between individual counterparties.

Example 3.1   Variation margin.

The diagrams show a 1-month repo for the term 23 December 2005 to 23 January 2006 where a margin of 2.00% is taken. The repo rate is 4.50%.

Bond is 5% 2012:

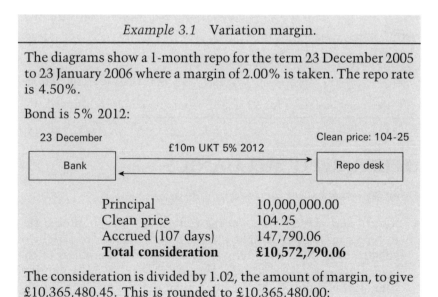

	Principal	10,000,000.00
	Clean price	104.25
	Accrued (107 days)	147,790.06
	Total consideration	**£10,572,790.06**

The consideration is divided by 1.02, the amount of margin, to give £10,365,480.45. This is rounded to £10,365,480.00:

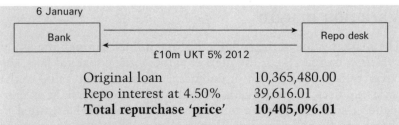

Original loan	10,365,480.00
Repo interest at 4.50%	39,616.01
Total repurchase 'price'	**10,405,096.01**

Assume now that half-way through the trade there has been a large drop in the bond market and the 5% 2012 gilt is trading down at 101.75. Following this drop in market price the securities are now worth:

Principal	10,000,000.00
Accrued (121 days)	167,127.07
Total	**£10,342,127.07**

The repo desk has however lent £10,365,480.00 against this security. It therefore calls for variation margin from the counter-party in the form of eligible securities or cash.

To restore the original margin of 2.00% the repo desk would call for an adjustment calculated as follows:

$$\left[\left(\begin{array}{c} \text{Original} \\ \text{consideration} \end{array} + \begin{array}{c} \text{Repo interest accrued} \\ \text{on consideration} \end{array} \right) \times (1 + \text{Initial margin}) \right]$$
$$- (\text{New all-in price} \times \text{Nominal amount})$$

This therefore becomes:

$$[(10,365,480.00 + 19,337.01) \times 1.02]$$
$$-(1.0342127 \times 10,000,000) = \pounds 250,386.35$$

So, the margin call is for £250,386 from the collateral provider.

OTHER REPO MECHANICS

Other repo mechanics we need to note are:

- *Return and substitution* – at the time of dealing, counterparties to repo can agree to a right of return early, and/or to a right of substitution. The first involves breaking the loan ahead of the agreed maturity date, usually because the collateral is required back. If this right has been agreed, then there is no issue and the loan is matured early. The cost for having this right is usually a repo rate that is 1 or 2 basis points higher than the normal rate. A right of substitution means that the borrower of cash can call back collateral during the term of the trade, as long as he replaces it with collateral of equal quality. Generally, this means a government bond would need to be replaced with another government bond, or a AAA-rated MBS would need to be replaced with a AAA-rated MBS. Substitution can be unlimited or limited to a specified number during the term of the trade.

• *Mark-to-market* – at the start of the trade the collateral is priced and this is used to calculate its market value, which then drives the amount of the cash lent. During the term of the trade the collateral is regularly marked-to-market, which can then lead to margin calls. Counterparties can use a third-party price, often the cash lender will obtain a price or ask the cash borrower to supply a price.

• *Maturity* – the standard repo trade is dealt with a specified, fixed maturity date. An *open* repo is one in which either (a) no maturity date is specified, in which case it is renewed as required each morning or (b) the maturity date is set at 1, 2, 3 years or even longer, but the repo is renewed (and the rate re-set) at regular intervals, such as daily, monthly or quarterly. At each renew date either side has the right to terminate the repo.

REPO DEALING RISKS

A knowledge of repo dealing risks is required for a full understanding of what is behind repo mechanics. We introduce the most significant risks here.

Interdependent risks

As with all capital market transactions there are risks attached to trading in repo. These risks can be grouped into the following areas:

• credit risk/counterparty risk;
• legal risk;
• collateral risk/issuer risk;
• market risk;
• daylight exposure;
• systems and controls (operational risk).

In certain cases the risk exposure by a market counterparty will be a function of more than one of the above; hence, we refer to these risks as being interdependent.

Financial market risks

Generally, credit risk, issuer risk, legal risk and market risk can be thought of as functions of counterparty risk, as opposed to operational risk which is generally an internal issue (unless a firm is affected by operational weakness in a counterparty).

Credit risk

This is the risk that the counterparty defaults on the transaction, due to financial difficulty or going out of business entirely. Although this is a serious issue, it is more so for unsecured creditors of the company, including those who have dealt in (unsecured) interbank transactions with the company. A market participant that has entered into a repo transaction may feel that he is protected by the collateral he is holding.

Banks and other market participants guard against credit risk by internally rating all their counterparties, and assigning trading limits to each of them. The trading limit may be higher for repo than interbank trading, or set at the same level. In some cases counterparties deemed unsuitable for an interbank limit are not assigned secured lending limits either; an example of this occurred after the collapse of the Barings merchant bank in 1995. Many UK building societies withdrew or drastically reduced limits for other similar merchant banks in the unsecured market. This continued to be the case when the gilt repo market was introduced the following year, despite the quality of collateral involved in this market.

Credit ratings

The different credit ratings of market participants are reflected in the rates paid by each of them in the debt market. This is illustrated diagrammatically in Figure 3.4.

Table 3.1 summarises the long-term corporate bond ratings assigned by the main international credit rating agencies.

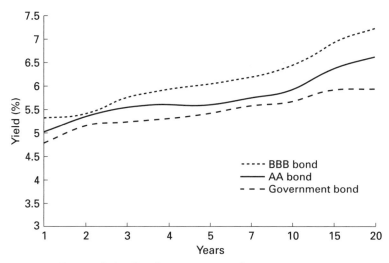

Figure 3.4 Credit structure of interest rates.

Although the rating agencies specify all paper at the level of Baa3/ BBB– and above as being of 'investment grade', in practice often only banks and corporates rated at Baa1/BBB+ or higher are deemed suitable counterparties for unsecured transactions.

Issuer risk

This refers also to collateral risk, the risk that the quality of collateral held will suffer because the fortunes of the issuer decline. For this reason many repo market participants will only accept AAA-rated paper, such as government bonds, as collateral. In the case of equity repo usually only blue-chip shares are accepted (e.g., the shares of FTSE 100 or S&P 500 companies). The market for lower quality collateral is less liquid, and the equivalent GC rate will be higher than that for government collateral, reflecting the higher risk involved. In the UK the equity repo rate typically trades at around 35–50 basis points over the government rate.

Market risk

Market risk is the risk of a change in the value of an asset due to moves in market levels/prices. Repo market participants are exposed to movements in interest rates during the course of each transaction. They are also exposed to changes in the value of collateral.

Table 3.1   Long-term corporate bond credit ratings.

Fitch	Moody	S&P	Summary description
			Investment grade–high creditworthiness
AAA	Aaa	AAA	Gilt-edged, prime, maximum safety, lowest risk
AA+ AA AA−	Aa1 Aa2 Aa3	AA+ AA AA−	} High-grade, high credit quality
A+ A A−	A1 A2 A3	A+ A A−	} Upper-medium grade
BBB+ BBB BBB−	Baa1 Baa2 Baa3	BBB+ BBB BBB−	} Lower-medium grade

Fitch	Moody	S&P	Summary description
			Speculative–lower creditworthiness
BB+ BB BB−	Ba1 Ba2 Ba3	BB+ BB BB−	} Low grade; speculative
B+ B B−	B1 B B3	B	} Highly speculative

Fitch	Moody	S&P	Summary description
			Predominantly speculative, substantial risk or in default
CCC+ CCC	Caa	CCC+ CCC	} Substantial risk, in poor standing
CC C	Ca C	CC C CI	} May be in default, very speculative Extremely speculative Income bonds – no interest being paid
DDD DD D		D	} Default

One reason for the continuing popularity of the stock lending market is because lenders, such as fund managers and insurance companies, prefer to lend stock in return for a fixed fee rather that engage in repo, which requires a dealing desk and interest-rate management and exposes the lender to market risk.

Changes in the value of collateral are the main reason for engaging in *margining* in repo transactions.

Dealing with risk

The issue of credit risk is still relevant in a secured transaction, such as repo. There may be an inclination to attach a lower level of importance compared with an unsecured transaction.

A holding of collateral may still create problems in the event of default, as the lender of cash may not have legal title to the collateral, or a sufficient amount of collateral. When a counterparty is in default, the process of liquidation or administration can be a lengthy one; it also may not be possible to enforce ownership through legal title, as other creditors may be 'ahead of the queue'. This is an example of *insolvency risk*, as the liquidator may be able to cherry-pick the assets of the company, which may include the assets held by the repo counterparty.

Ultimately, the most effective means of dealing with the various risks is to 'know your counterparty'. Some market participants go further and only engage in repo with firms with whom they would also deal in the unsecured market.

Reducing legal risk

There has been some progress in reducing the legal risk exposure in repo trading. These include:

- a formal, binding, legal agreement, of which the BMA/ICMA agreement is the best example (see Chapter 8). In the UK gilt repo market, for example, parties are required to sign this document before being able to commence dealing. A participant has to have the signed agreement in place with each counterparty it deals with;
- the International Stock Lenders Association (*OSLA*) agreement;
- standard domestic agreements (such as the *pension livrée* in France).

Default arrangements

Most markets have provision for a set-off mechanism in the event of default, known as 'netting'. This means that:

- all outstanding loans/repos are recalled or repurchased;
- each party's obligations to the other are valued and converted into a monetary amount;
- the resulting cash sums are set off and only the net balance is payable by the party owing the greater amount.

Reducing collateral risk

We have stated that the common response to exposure to market risk is to include the practice of *margining*. In order for margin calls to take place, market participants have to engage in *marking-to-market* of all their positions. A bond would be marked at its current market price at the close of business. Where the value has fallen by a predetermined amount, the lender of cash will ask for margin.

This is not a water-tight arrangement in the event of default. The cash lender may still find herself short of a sufficient amount of collateral, due to the following:

- there may have been adverse market movements between the last margin call and payment;
- there may be an element of *concentration risk*, associated with illiquid issues, where the lender is holding a high proportion of bonds from the same issuer, which then become illiquid and difficult to realise.

A solution to this potential problem is to engage in daily margin calls.

SELECTED REFERENCE

Choudhry, M. (2005). *The Money Markets Handbook*. John Wiley & Sons.

Chapter

4

....

BASKET REPO, SYNTHETIC REPO AND STRUCTURED FINANCE REPO

The repo examples considered earlier were all single-name repos. In this chapter we consider basket repo, which is a repo of a portfolio of bonds. We also look at total return swaps, which are economically a form of repo and sometimes called 'synthetic repo', and the use of repo in structured finance vehicles known as 'conduits'.

BASKET REPO

Banks, securities houses and hedge funds often repo out entire portfolios of bonds with a repo market maker. This is known as a *basket repo* and is operationally more convenient because it is treated as one repo trade rather than a large number of individual bond repo trades. Such treatment makes the cash flows easier from an operational point of view. The mechanics of a basket repo are identical to that for a single-name bond classic repo.

Illustration of basket repo trade: Malaysian Government securities

We assume a securities house buys the current three Malaysian Government international bonds that are denominated in US dollars.

Table 4.1 shows the three bonds and the cash flows associated with financing them. Imagine the securities house, ABC Securities Limited, wishes to fund them using repo. It arranges a basket repo with an investment bank, with the following terms:

Trade date	28 May 2004
Value date	3 June 2004
Repo maturity date	30 August 2005
Interest reset	1 month
Wired proceeds	USD 27,043,002.10
Rate	1.33 (1-month Libor fix of 27 May 2004 plus 22 bps)
Interest	USD 32,969.93
Maturity proceeds	USD 27,075,972.03

Note that the investment bank that is entering into a basket reverse repo has applied a margin or haircut to each security, depending on what credit rating the security is assigned. The following margin

Table 4.1 Hypothetical portfolio of Malaysian Government bonds, securities house basket repo trade.

Bond	ISIN	Type	Nominal value (USD)	Credit rating	Price	Accrued interest	Market value	Haircut (%)	Loan value (USD)
Malaysia FLOAT July 2007	XS0149973850	Sovereign FRN	5,000,000	Baa1/A−	99.98	44,906.00	5,043,906.00	5.00	4,791,710.70
Malaysia 8.75% June 2009	US560904AE46	Sovereign	10,000,000	Baa1/A−	118.44	4,861.00	11,848,921.00	5.00	11,256,474.95
Malaysia July 2001	US560904AF11	Sovereign	10,000,000	Baa1/A−	112.85	287,500.00	11,573,491.00	5.00	10,994,816.45
							28,466,318.00		**27,043,002.10**
									Repo basket amount 'wired proceeds'

Price source: Bloomberg L.P. Prices as at 28 May 2004.

levels can be assumed for haircut levels in this market:

AAA to AA	2.0%
A	3.5%
BBB	5%
Sub-investment grade	10%

The repo is booked as one trade, even though the securities house is repoing out three different bonds. It has a 3-month formal term, but its interest rate is reset every month. The first interest period rate is set as 1-month London Interbank Offered Rate (Libor) plus a spread of 22 basis points, which is 1.33%.

The trade can be 'broken' at that date, or rolled for another month. Table 4.2 shows the trade ticket.

During the term of the trade, the market maker will make a margin call at pre-agreed intervals – say, weekly or every fortnight. This is done by revaluing the entire basket and, if the portfolio has declined in value, a margin call will be made to restore the balance of the haircut. Table 4.3 shows a margin call statement for 1 week after initial value date; we assume the portfolio has declined in value and, hence, a margin payment will need to be made by ABC Securities Limited.

As the trade is conducted under a standard legal agreement, the securities house will be able to substitute bonds out of the basket if it wishes, provided securities of equivalent quality are sent in the place of any bonds taken out of the basket.

Table 4.2   Basket repo trade ticket, investment bank
market maker.

Reverse repo (RR)	*Contract*	
Customer ID	123456789	ABC Securities Limited
Contract amount	$27,043,002.10	
Rate (fixed)	1.330 00%	
Settle date	03-Jun-04	
Lock-up date	06-Jul-04	
Total repo principal	$27,043,002.10	
Total repo interest	$32,969.93	
Due at maturity	$27,075,972.03	
Number of pieces	3	

Table 4.3   Margin call statement: fixed income financing margin call.

Date	08-Jun-04
Valuation date	10-Jun-04
Due date	14-Jun-04
Positive number =	Amount receivable
Negative number =	Amount payable
Exposure	(27,043,002.10)
Haircut amount	1,423,315.90
Portfolio revaluation	(26,593,002.10)
Margin call	450,000.00

Illustration using structured finance securities

The same principles are demonstrated in this example of a basket repo trade where the collateral is composed of structured finance securities, such as ABS, MBS and collateralised debt obligations.

Table 4.4 shows a very small portfolio of five structured finance bonds, a mix of ABS, MBS and CDO notes. Imagine that these are held by a securities house, ABC Securities Limited, that wishes to fund them using repo. It arranges a basket repo with an investment bank, with the following terms:

Trade date	13 February 2004
Value date	17 February 2004
Maturity date	17 February 2005
Interest reset	3 months
Wired proceeds	USD 45,564,607.50
Rate	1.18188 (3-month Libor fix of 12 February 2004 plus 6 bps)
Interest	USD 134,629.75
Maturity proceeds	USD 45,699,237.25

Note that the investment bank that is entering into a basket reverse repo has applied a margin or haircut to each security, depending on what credit rating the security is assigned. The following margin

Table 4.4 Hypothetical portfolio of ABS bonds, securities house basket repo trade.

Bond	CUSIP	Type	Asset type	Nominal value (USD)	Credit rating	Pool factor	Price	Market value	Haircut (%)	Loan value (USD)
ABCMT 2003-B B	00761HAU5	ABS	Credit card	10,000,000	A	1.00	102.125	10,212,500.00	5.00	9,701,875.00
ACAS 2002-2A B	00080AAL4	ABS	Small business loans	5,000,000	A	1.00	102.25	5,112,500.00	5.00	4,856,875.00
AMSI 2003-1 M2	03072SEZ4	MBS	Home equity	8,500,000	A	1.00	102.25	8,691,250.00	5.00	8,256,687.50
AMSI 2003-IA1 M2	03072SLH6	ABS	Residential B/C	4,000,000	A	1.00	102.5	4,100,000.00	5.00	3,895,000.00
Indosuez Capital Funding III	45578YAA0	CLO	Commercial bank loans	20,000,000	AA	1.00	97.69	19,538,000.00	3.50	18,854,170.00
								47,654,250.00		**45,564,607.50**
										Repo basket amount

Price source: Bloomberg L.P. Prices as at 12 February 2004.

Table 4.5   Basket repo trade ticket, investment bank
market maker.

Reverse repo (RR)	Contract	
Customer ID	123456789	ABC Securities Limited
Contract amount	$45,564,607.50	
Rate (fixed)	1.181 88%	
Settle date	17-Feb-04	
Lock-up date	17-May-04	
Total repo principal	$45,564,607.50	
Total repo interest	$134,629.75	
Due at maturity	$45,699,237.25	
Number of pieces	5	

levels can be assumed for haircut levels in this trade:

AAA to AA	3.5%
A	5%
BBB	7%
Sub-investment grade	10%

The repo is booked as one trade, even though the securities house is repoing out five different bonds. It has a 1-year formal term, but its interest rate is reset every quarter. The first interest period rate is set as 3-month Libor plus a spread of 6 basis points. The trade can be 'broken' at that date, or rolled for another 3 months. Table 4.5 shows the trade ticket.

During the term of the trade, the market maker will make a margin call at pre-agreed intervals – say, weekly or every fortnight. This is done by revaluing the entire basket and, if the portfolio has declined in value, a margin call will be made to restore the balance of the haircut. Table 4.6 shows a margin call statement for 1 week after initial value date; we assume the portfolio has declined in value and, hence, a margin payment will need to be made by ABC Securities Limited.

As the trade is conducted under the Global Master Repurchase Agreement (GMRA), the securities house will be able to substitute bonds out of the basket if it wishes, provided securities of equivalent quality are sent in the place of any bonds taken out of the basket.

Table 4.6 Margin call statement: fixed
income financing margin call.

Date	24-Feb-04
Valuation date	23-Feb-04
Due date	24-Feb-04
Positive number =	Amount receivable
Negative number =	Amount payable
Exposure	**(45,564,607.50)**
Haircut amount	2,089,642.50
Portfolio revaluation	47,224,291.50
Margin call	429,958.50

SYNTHETIC REPO VIA THE TOTAL RETURN SWAP

Synthetic repo, undertaken for the purposes of funding a portfolio or borrowing stocks to cover short positions, is common in the market. The repo is in the form of a total return swap (TRS), which is classified as a credit derivative instrument; however, when traded for funding or stock borrowing purposes, it is identical in economic terms to a classic repo. TRS contracts are used in a variety of applications by banks; further detail on them is available in Choudhry (2004).

When used for funding purposes, a TRS is more akin to a synthetic repo contract.[1] To illustrate this application, we describe here the use of TRS to fund a portfolio of bonds, as a substitute for a repo trade.[2]

---

[1] The economic effect may be the same, but they are considered different instruments. TRS actually takes the assets off the balance sheet, whereas the tax and accounting authorities treat repo as if the assets remain on the balance sheet. In addition, a TRS trade is conducted under the ISDA standard legal agreement, while repo is conducted under the GMRA standard repo legal agreement. It is these differences that, under certain circumstances, make the TRS funding route a more favourable one.

[2] There may be legal, administrative, operational or other reasons why a repo trade is not entered into to begin with. In these cases, provided that a counterparty can be found and the funding rate is not prohibitive, a TRS may be just as suitable.

Consider a financial institution such as a regulated broker-dealer that has a portfolio of assets on its balance sheet for which it needs to obtain funding. These assets are investment-grade rated structured finance bonds – such as credit card ABS, residential MBS and CDO notes – and investment-grade rated convertible bonds. In the repo market, it is able to fund these at Libor plus 16 basis points. That is, it can repo the bonds out to a bank counterparty, and will pay Libor plus 16 basis points on the funds it receives.

Assume that for operational reasons the bank can no longer fund these assets using repo. Instead, it can fund them using a basket TRS contract, providing a suitable counterparty can be found. Under this contract, the portfolio of assets is swapped out to the TRS counterparty and cash received from the counterparty. The assets are therefore sold off the balance sheet to the counterparty, an investment bank. The investment bank will need to fund this itself – it may have a line of credit from a parent bank or it may swap the bonds out into the market. The funding rate it charges the broker-dealer will depend to a large extent on what rate the bank can fund the assets itself. Assume that the TRS rate charged is Libor plus 22 basis points – the higher rate reflects the lower liquidity in the basket TRS market for non-vanilla bonds.

The portfolio is shown at Table 4.7. At the start of the trade, the portfolio consists of five (hypothetical) EUR-denominated convertible bonds. The broker-dealer enters into a 3-month TRS with the investment bank counterparty, with a 1-week interest-rate reset. This means at each 1-week interval the basket is revalued. The difference in value from the last valuation is paid (if higher) or received (if lower) by the investment bank to the broker-dealer; in return, the broker-dealer also pays 1-week interest on the funds it received at the start of the trade. The trade can be broken at 1-week intervals and bonds in the reference basket can be returned, added to or substituted. So, if any stocks have been sold or bought, they can be removed or added to the basket on the reset date. If the bonds have not moved in price between the reset dates, then there is no performance for the investment bank to make.

The terms of the trade are:

Trade date	24 March 2004
Value date	26 March 2004
Maturity date	28 June 2004
Rate reset	31 March 2004
Interest rate	2.2970% (this is a 1-week EUR Libor fix of 2.077% plus 16 bps)

Table 4.7 Basket TRS trade on 24 March 2004, undertaken for funding purposes.

TRS ticket							
EUR€ 1W Libor	2.077						

Name	Currency	Nominal	Price	Accrued	Pool factor	Consideration (€)	ISIN code
ABC Telecoms 6.25%	EUR	11,000,000	113.50	0.024 658	N/A	12,487,712.38	XS ----------
SPG Bros 7.50%	EUR	10,000,000	136.29	0.519 444	N/A	13,680,944.40	XS ----------
KFC/DTI 5.875%	EUR	35,000,000	104.63	0.469 262	N/A	36,784,741.70	XS ----------
Bigenddi 8.25%	EUR	15,000,000	122.48	0.000 000	N/A	18,372,000.00	XS ----------
BanglaTown 9%	EUR	50,000,000	41.95	1.471 875	N/A	21,151,625.00	XS ----------
Jackfruit Funding ABS (addition to basket at roll-over)	**EUR**	**5,000,000**	**99.95**	**0.000 000**	**1.000 000**	**4,997,500.00**	**XS ----------**

102,477,023.48

Portfolio value at start

107,474,523.48

Portfolio value at roll-over

Start of loan	
Portfolio additions (€)	0.00
Loan amount (€)	102,477,023.48
Interest rate	2.297 000%

Roll-over payments

Interest (€)

Rate   2.297 000%
Principal   102,477,023.48

Interest payable   **−45,770.22**

Performance ($)

Portfolio additions (€)	4,997,500.00
Accrued interest	57,671.16
Price movements	0.00
New portfolio value	107,532,194.64
Old portfolio value	102,477,023.48

Performance payment   +5,055,171.16

Net payment (€)
Broker-dealer receives from bank   **+5,009,400.94**

New loan

Portfolio additions (€)	4,997,500.00
New loan amount (€)	107,532,194.64
New interest rate	2.252 880%

The combined market value of the entire portfolio is taken to be EUR 102,477,023.48. There is no haircut.

At the start of the trade, the five bonds are swapped out to the investment bank, who pays the portfolio value for them. On the first reset date, the portfolio is revalued and the following calculations confirmed:

Old portfolio value	EUR 102,477,023.48
Interest rate	2.2970%
Interest payable by broker-dealer	EUR 45,770.22.
New portfolio value	EUR 107,532,194.64
Portfolio performance	+5,055,171.16
Net payment: broker-dealer receives	EUR 5,009,400.94

These values are shown at Table 4.7. There has been no change in the prices of the five convertible bonds, but the broker-dealer has added an ABS security to the portfolio. In addition, there has been 1 week's accrued interest on the original portfolio. This makes up the new portfolio value.

The rate is reset for value 2 April 2004 for the period to 9 April 2004. The new rate is 22 basis points over the 1-week EUR Libor fix on 31 March 2004, an all-in rate of 2.252 880%. This interest rate is payable on the new 'loan' amount of EUR 107,532,194.64.

This trade has the same goals and produced the same economic effect as a classic repo transaction.

STRUCTURED FUNDING VEHICLES: REPO CONDUIT

Banks and other financial institutions make increasing use of more structured vehicles as they strive to create more efficient mechanisms to raise funds and generate liquidity. In this section we describe some of the latest structures worked on by the author in the US dollar and euro markets.

Securities repo conduit

There are various forms of a repo-based structured funding vehicle that provides efficient funding of securities portfolio known as a 'securities repo conduit'. This is used to provide funding for a wide range of assets including residential mortgages, commercial mortgages, structured finance securities – such as student loan ABS – and existing conduit vehicles.[3] It is an on-balance sheet funding mechanism, and is similar to a commercial paper (CP) conduit, but with added flexibility both on its asset and liability side. It provides access to the CP market but without requirement of a back-up bank liquidity facility, because the conduit is supported by the pool of assets that are being financed. As such, it enables the originator to reduce its reliance on CP and repo dealers, while also guaranteeing access to the market during times of market disruption.

Structure

The securities repo conduit is essentially a means by which an investment bank, via a separate legal entity or via its own balance sheet, will provide a 'warehouse' funding vehicle for a client that wishes to finance a pool of assets.

The structure is designed as follows:

A separate legal entity – special purpose entity or special purpose vehicle (SPV) – is set up as a bankruptcy-remote funding vehicle, which is the issuer. Thereafter:

- the issuer issues short-term notes, termed 'loan notes' or 'asset-backed loan notes' (ABNs) that are issued at A-1/P-1/F-1 or better,[4] which are backed by repo agreements between it and the client entity;
- the client repo's securities between it and the issuer, which act as the collateral for the ABNs. The amount of collateral will be equal to the value of notes issued plus an additional amount as credit enhancement;
- the repo provides sufficient funds to pay off the ABNs on maturity, with the repo and ABNs being set with identical maturities;
- the repo between the issuer and the client will allow for the repo securities (collateral) to be bankruptcy-remote from the fortunes of the client.

In effect, the ABNs are a repo-backed funding issue rather than a pure asset-backed note issue. It is the repo that provides the security for

---

[3] See Choudhry (2004) for background on commercial paper conduits.
[4] The top S&P and Fitch short-term credit ratings are A-1+ and F-1+.

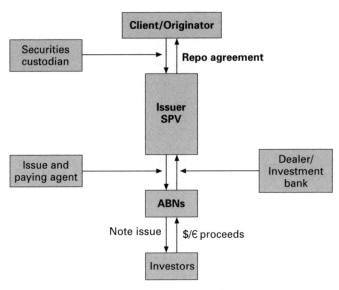

Figure 4.1   Securities repo conduit structure.

the ABNs, rather than the underlying securities themselves. So, the cash flow patterns of the underlying securities, whatever type they are, are not strictly relevant to the security-backing of an ABN issue.

Figure 4.1 shows the structure diagram.

The terms of an ABN issue might look something like this:

Instrument type	Discount paper
Maturity	30–270 days (USD); 364 days (EUR, GBP)
Legal final maturity	[30] days after expected final maturity
Rate:	Libor minus [5–7] basis points (excluding dealer fee)
Repo terms:	Equal nominal value plus haircut Identical maturity date

The repo agreement is entered into simultaneously with any ABN issue, and is the security backing for the ABN.

Credit enhancement

A key element of securitisation technology is the concept of credit enhancement, which is set to achieve the required credit rating. A securities repo conduit will employ one or both methods of credit

Table 4.8   Example of haircut value for security type (%).

Maturity	RMBS		CMBS		Credit card ABS		Manufactured housing	
	Aaa	Aa2	Aaa	Aa2	Aaa	Aa2	Aaa	Aa2
1 year	3.4	3.9	3.4	4.1	3.1	3.7	4.8	5.6
5 years	15.5	16.3	15.7	17.8	13.7	15.5	17.0	22.1
10 years	19.1	21.2	21.4	24.3	17.4	19.6	21.0	26.5

Source: Moody's. Reproduced with permission.

enhancement – namely, over-collateralisation and a swap arrangement.

With over-collateralisation, the market value of the securities assigned under the repo agreement is set at a higher level of the nominal value of the ABN issue. This value is the margin or 'haircut'. The size of the haircut is based on the following:

• credit quality of securities being repoed;
• overall market liquidity;
• historical price volatility of collateral securities.

The repo side of the transaction is marked-to-market on a regular basis and additional collateral will be called for if the haircut value falls during the term of the trade. An indication of the size of expected haircut for different classes of security is shown at Table 4.8, which shows the levels described by Moody's.

The other method of credit enhancement is a swap arrangement. Under this, a swap counterparty that is rated at least A-1+/P-1/F-1+ and AA−/AA−/Aa3 will be contracted to cover the market risk of the collateral. The swap is set for a fixed term – say, 3–5 years; at all times the notional value of the swap will be equal to the total value of outstanding collateral in the repo facility. The maximum such size is the total issuance under the conduit.

The swap payment profile under a regular-setting market value swap is:

• the issuer pays to the swap counterparty any upside performance received from sale of securities;
• the swap counterparty pays to the issuer any shortfall in the market value of the securities incurred by the sale of said securities.

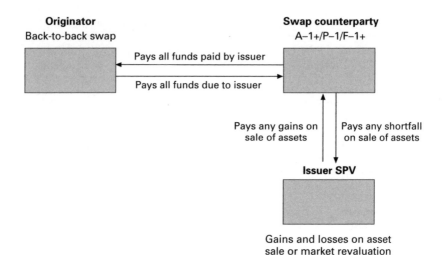

Figure 4.2   Securities repo conduit, swap arrangement: structure of cash flows.

A mirror arrangement is put in place between the swap counterparty and both the originator and the issuer.

The swap cash flows are shown at Figure 4.2.

SELECTED REFERENCE

Choudhry, M. (2004). *Structured Credit Products: Credit Derivatives and Synthetic Securitisation*. John Wiley & Sons.

Chapter

5

THE UK GILT REPO MARKET

The UK gilt repo market is worth looking at in detail because it is a rare example (possibly the only example) of a market that was established fully-formed at birth. The Bank of England (*BoE*), after market consultation, set out the market structure in advance and the market was established ready to deal and settle on 2 January 1996. In other words, a 'big bang' inception date was set and market trading began as planned on that date. It has proved a considerable success, and is a good illustration of how to introduce new structures into an existing capital market.[1]

INTRODUCTION

Prior to this, stock borrowing and lending in the gilt market was available only to gilt-edged market makers (*GEMMs*), dealing through approved intermediaries – that is, stock exchange money brokers (*SEMBs*). The introduction of gilt repo allowed all market participants to borrow and lend gilts. Market reforms also liberalised gilt stock lending by removing the restrictions on who could borrow and lend stock, thus ensuring a 'level playing field' between the two types of transaction. The gilt-edged stock lending agreement (*GESLA*) was also updated to ensure that it dovetailed with the new gilt repo legal agreement; the revised GESLA was issued in December 1995 and repo and stock lending are inter-linked aspects of the new, open market.

In the run-up to the start of repo trading, market practitioners and regulators drew up recommended market practices, set out in the *Gilt Repo Code of Best Practice*. The associated legal agreement is the Bond Market Association (*BMA*)/International Capital Markets Association (*ICMA*) Global Master Repurchase Agreement (*GMRA*), with an addendum to cover the special features of gilts, such as the use of delivery by value (*DBV*) within the Central Gilts Office (*CGO*) (now CREST) settlement mechanism.

---

[1] As ever, thanks to Derek Taylor at King & Shaxson Limited, this time for that day back in January 1996 when, on a query from the author, he reminded him gilt repo price quotes were like CD quotes, bid–offer. In the case of repo, one bids for stock, so lends the cash . . .

Growth of market

The market grew to about £50 billion of repos and stock lending outstanding in its first 2 months. Further growth took it to nearly £95 billion by February 1997, of which £70 billion was in repos. This figure fell to about £75 billion by November 1998, compared with £100 billion for sterling certificates of deposit (*CDs*). As at November 2005 the figure was over £90 billion. Data collected on turnover by

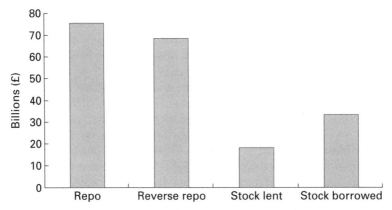

Figure 5.1   Repo market volume November 2005.
Source: Bank of England.

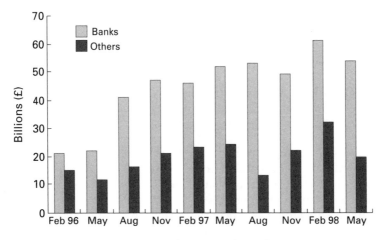

Figure 5.2   Repo market growth in first 2 years.
Source: Bank of England.

the Bank suggest that average daily turnover in gilt repo was around £22 billion in November 2005.

Gilt repo and other sterling money markets

Gilt repo developed alongside growth in the existing unsecured money markets. Its introduction led to a visible shift in short-term money market trading patterns from unsecured to secured money. According to the BoE market participants estimate that gilt repo now accounts for over half of all overnight transactions in the sterling money markets. For some time after the introduction of the market, the repo general collateral (GC) rate always traded below the inter-bank rate, on average about 10–15 basis points below, reflecting its status as government credit. The gap was less obvious at very short maturities, due to the lower value of such credit over the short term and also reflecting the higher demand for short-term funding through repo by securities houses that may not have access to unsecured money. However, more recently the repo rate has not always traded below London Interbank Offered Rate (Libor), although given its status as risk-free collateral in theory it would always be expected to. Figure 5.3, which is a page from the Bloomberg graph tool 'G' <go>, shows the spread between the 1-month Libor rate and the 1-month GC repo rate as reported by the British Bankers Association for the period December 2004–December 2005. We see that on occasion – for example, during July 2005 – the repo rate traded with the Libor rate. This is surprising and must reflect supply and demand factors.

Figure 5.4 shows the same spread, this time for the 1-week rate.

The CD market has grown substantially, partly because the growth of the gilt repo and stock lending market has contributed to demand for CDs for use as collateral in stock loans.

One effect of gilt repo on the money market is a possible association with a reduction in the volatility of overnight unsecured rates. Fluctuations in the overnight unsecured market have been reduced since the start of an open repo market, although the evidence is not conclusive. This may be due to repo providing an alternative funding method for market participants, which may have reduced pressure on the unsecured market in overnight funds. It may also have enhanced the ability of financial intermediaries to distribute liquidity.

Figure 5.3 Bloomberg screen 'G' showing 1-month Libor rate minus 1-month gilt repo GC rate, December 2004–December 2005.

© Bloomberg L.P. Used with permission. Visit *www.bloomberg.com*

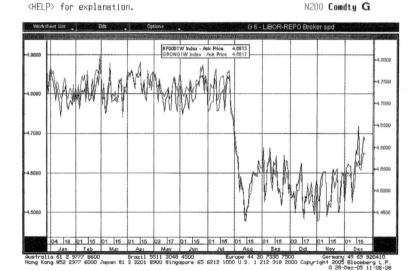

Figure 5.4 Bloomberg screen 'G' showing 1-week Libor rate minus 1-month gilt repo GC rate, December 2004–December 2005.

© Bloomberg L.P. Used with permission. Visit *www.bloomberg.com*

IMPACT ON THE GILT MARKET

The main objective in introducing gilt repo was to enhance the liquidity of the gilt market and the attraction of gilts, particularly to overseas investors. There is some evidence that liquidity has improved, with firms able to transact deals in larger size than previously without moving market prices or spreads against them, and an indicated reduction in the spread of gilt prices from GEMMs.

Gilt repo has also contributed to improvements in the gilt-edged market making function. The possibility of undertaking gilt repo with any counterparty has enhanced the ability of market makers (GEMMs) to make markets in gilts, by improving their access to stock to cover short positions and lessening the cost of so doing, and by reducing the cost of financing their long positions, from above Libor to below Libid. The average cost of borrowing stock has also fallen, according to the BoE. These lower financing and borrowing costs are also available to other market participants. On anecdotal evidence it would appear that gilts are now less likely to trade at anomalous prices, and data from the BoE indicates that the divergence of GEMM-quoted yields from its own fitted yield curve has decreased. However, it is difficult to strip out other factors contributing to developments such as these; for instance, the extremely competitive world of gilts market making would also appear to have contributed to gilt prices and quote spreads becoming very keen.

The ability of all market participants to short gilts and to take and finance or cover their desired positions has improved the efficiency and liquidity of the gilt market. There is anecdotal evidence that larger size bargains are easier to accomplish and that the spread of gilt prices has been reduced. The development of a liquid market in secured money has widened the range of funding and money placement options open to financial and non-financial firms. It may also be associated with a reduction in volatility of overnight interest rates.

These developments in sterling markets all contribute to the market's positive perception of the gilt market and to the willingness of investors both at home and abroad to invest in gilts. The ultimate beneficiary will be the economy itself through a reduction in the cost of public borrowing as a direct result of reforms such as the introduction of open repo.

MARKET STRUCTURE
Repo and stock lending

The UK market structure comprises both gilt repo and gilt stock lending. Some institutions will trade in one activity, although of course many firms will engage in both. Although there are institutions which undertake only one type of activity, there are many institutions trading actively in both areas. For example, an institution that is short of a particular gilt may cover its short position (which could result from either an outright sale or a repo) in either the gilt repo or the stock lending market.

Certain institutions prefer to use repo because they feel that the value of a *special* stock is more rapidly and more accurately reflected in the repo than the stock lending market. Some firms have preferred to remain in stock lending because their existing systems and control procedures can accommodate stock lending more readily than repo. For example, a firm may have no cash re-investment facility or experience of managing interest-rate risk. Such a firm will prefer to receive collateral against a stock loan for a fee, rather than interest bearing cash in a repo. They may also feel that their business does not need or cannot justify the costs of setting up a repo trading facility. In addition, stock lending has benefited from securities houses and banks who trade in both it and repo; for example, borrowing a stock in the lending market, repoing this and then investing the cash in, say, the CD market.

Other firms have embraced repo due, for instance, to the perception that value from tight stock is more readily obtained in the repo market than in the lending market.

Market participants: market making in repo

Virtually from the start of the market some firms have provided what is in effect a market making function in gilt repo. Typical of these are the former SEMBs and banks that run large matched books. According to the BoE there are around 20 firms, mostly banks and securities houses, which quote two-way repo rates on request for GC, specifics and specials, up to 3months. Longer maturities may also sometimes be readily quoted.

At the start of the market, former SEMBs such as Gerrard & National and Lazards, Rowe & Pitman (now part of the UBS group) took part as market makers; however, such firms have largely disappeared from the market or been subsumed into larger banking groups. Market makers are now banks such as Royal Bank of Scotland (which absorbed NatWest Markets), Barclays Capital, HSBC, Deutsche Bank and CIBC. Some firms will quote only to established customers, such as ABN AMRO Securities Ltd. Some firms will quote indicative repo rates on screen services such as Reuters and Bloomberg – for example, the HBOS repo rates screen was shown in Chapter 1.

Market participants: brokers

A number of sterling broking houses are active in gilt repo. Counterparties still require signed legal documentation to be in place with each other, along with credit lines, before trading can take place. This is not the case in the interbank broking market. A gilt repo agreement is not required with the broker, although of course firms will have counterparty agreements in place with them. Typical of the firms providing broking services are Tullett & Tokyo and ICAP.

Brokers tend to specialise in different aspects of the gilt market. For example, some concentrate on GC repo, and others on *specials* and *specifics*; some on very short maturity transactions and others on longer term trades. Brokerage is usually 1 basis point of the total nominal amount of the bond transferred for GC, and 2 basis points for specific and special repo. Brokerage is paid by both sides to a gilt repo.

Market participants: end-users

The range of participants has grown as the market has expanded. The overall client base now includes banks, building societies, overseas banks and securities houses, hedge funds, fund managers (such as Standard Life, Scottish Amicable and so on), insurance companies and overseas central banks. Certain corporates have also begun to undertake gilt repo transactions. The slow start in the use of tri-party repo in the UK market has probably constrained certain corporates and smaller financial institutions from entering the market. Tri-party repo would be attractive to such institutions because of the lower administrative burden of having an external custodian. The largest users of gilt repo will remain banks and building societies, who are required to hold gilts as part of their BoE liquidity requirements.

GILT REPO AND THE YIELD CURVE

Impact of the yield curve

Generally, repo trading has been found to be more active when the yield curve is positively sloped, with overnight GC trading at lower rates than 1–2 weeks up to 1 month. This allows the repo trader to enjoy positive funding by borrowing cash overnight on repo while lending funds in the 1 week or 1 month. The trader is of course exposed to unexpected upward movements in overnight rates while covering his positions.

It should be remembered that the short-term money market curve acts independently of the cash gilt curve, especially with regard to long gilt yields, and often has nothing to do with its movements.

Example 5.1   Money market versus the bond market yield curve.

A good illustration of the low correlation in movement between the short-term money market yield curve and the gilt yield curve took place in summer 1997. Following the granting of interest-rate setting responsibility to the BoE, the gilt yield curve changed from a positive to a negative (inverted) curve; the Treasury 8% 2021 was yielding 6.54% in September 1997 and by December was yielding 6.37%. (The yield as at September 1998 was 5.15%.) Some firms' view was that the short-term curve would behave in the same manner. One market participant bid for 1-year GC at 7.18% at that time (September 1997), but by December 1997 this rate was 7.58%! An expensive trade ...

In this case the gilt yield curve had behaved as the trader had expected but the short-term money market curve had not.

[Market parlance: bid for stock – i.e., lend the cash.]

Hedging through repo

Hedging positions in other markets is one of the main motives for some participants' involvement in gilt repo. This is evident in the sterling bond market, where underwriters have benefited from the ability to hedge the interest-rate risk on their (long) underwriting positions, by taking an offsetting short position in the gilt they are using to price their bond. This improves the quality of their interest-rate hedge. The underwriter uses (reverse) repo to cover the short position in the gilt. Previously, underwriters that weren't GEMMs would have used less exact hedges such as the long gilt future.The introduction of open repo has therefore benefited the sterling bond market.

PATTERNS OF TRADING

Maturities

Gilt repo activity is concentrated at the very short end of the yield curve, with around 90% of trading at overnight to 1-week maturity. This is longer than stock lending, which is generally undertaken overnight or on call. As liquidity has improved, the volume – if not the proportion – of longer maturity trades has increased. Trades of up to 3 months' maturity are common, and 3-month repo rates are routinely quoted with a spread of around 5 basis points. Trades of up to 6 months are also not unusual.

Specials

The emergence of specials trading is a natural part of a repo market. One purpose in introducing a repo market was to allow the demand to borrow and lend stocks to be cleared by the price mechanism. Hence, it is natural that when stocks are in demand – for example, because firms wish to cover underwriting positions – the premium on obtaining them rises. Figure 5.5 shows the extent of specials premium for three gilt stocks at the start of 1997.

With the disappearance (on maturity) of exotic gilts and gilts with small issue sizes, specials activity has tended to dry up and is now quite rare. During November 2005 an enquiry to a broker suggested that only the 8% Treasury 2013 was special and trading at 'only' around 20 basis points through GC – suggesting that very few opportunities for specials trading presented themselves.

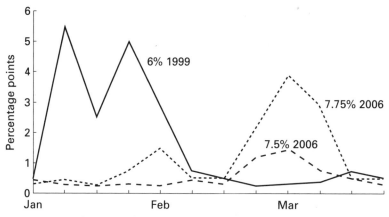

Figure 5.5 Gilt specials activity during 1997: 1-week special rates below the 1-week GC rate.

Example 5.2 Specials and the BoE.

On rare occasions, the Bank will intervene to relieve excess demand.

In November 1996 there was an increase in demand for 7.75% 2006, mainly because investors switched out of a similar maturity stock as it approached its ex-dividend period. Market makers sold the stock to meet this demand and then simultaneously covered their shorts in the repo market. This sudden demand coupled with the fact that a large amount of this issue was held by investors that did not lend it out led to the special rate trading at close to 0%. The Bank issued £100 million of the stock to help relieve demand.

For delivery into the March 1998 LIFFE long gilt futures contract, the BoE made supplies of the cheapest to deliver stock (Treasury 9% 2008) available if required, albeit at a rate of 0%!

The BoE has conducted a study into the relationship between cash prices and repo rates for stocks that have traded special. This showed a positive correlation between changes in a stock that trades expensive to the yield curve and changes in the degree to which it trades special. Theory would predict this: traders maintain short positions for paper which has high, associated funding costs only if the anticipated fall in the price of the paper is large enough to give a profit. (One implication of this is that longer duration stocks should be less expensive for a given specials premium, because their prices are more sensitive to changes in yields and therefore a given rise in yields will give a trader running a short position a higher profit to offset any increase in the cost of the repo.)

Both types of cause and effect can be explained:

- The stock may be perceived as expensive – for example, after an *auction* announcement. This creates a greater demand for short positions, and hence greater demand for the paper in repo (to cover short positions).
- At other times stock might go tight in the repo market. It would then tend to be bid higher in the *cash* market as traders closed out existing shorts, which were now too expensive to run; another reason would be that traders and *investors* would try to buy the stock outright since it would now be cheap to finance by repoing out.

The BoE has suggested that the link between dearness in the cash market and specialness in the repo market flows both ways: in some cases, changes in dearness have preceded changes in specialness and, in other cases, the sequence has been the other way round. In both cases the stock remains expensive until existing holders take profits by selling their stock or making it available for repo or lending.

GILTS SETTLEMENT AND CREST

Gilts, and gilt repo, was settled by the CGO, part of the BoE. The service was originally established in 1986 by the BoE and the London Stock Exchange to facilitate the settlement of specified securities, essentially gilts and certain sterling bonds such as bulldogs for which the BoE acts as registrar, and was upgraded by the BoE in 1997. In particular, the service was upgraded to enhance gilt repo trading activity, which commenced in January 1996, and to cater for the introduction of the gilt strips facility in December 1997. It also provides a vehicle for the development of real-time delivery versus payment (*DVP*) through links to the Real Time Gross Settlement System (*RTGS*) for wholesale payments, which was introduced in mid-1996.

CREST settlement

The CGO was merged with the equity settlement system CREST in 2002, and in 2003 this system was enhanced to settle gilt repo. In CREST, settlement of cash-driven repo against GC collateral takes place using the DBV system, which pre-dates the repo market and was the gilt settlement procedure.

Under this procedure, CREST delivers to the cash lender a basket of securities at a specified current market value, and meeting pre-defined criteria (such as gilts, or no index-linked gilts). DBVs settle at the end of each day and are unwound the next day. This makes them ideal for overnight trades and overnight repo, but results in large amounts of unwanted cash movements each day for term trades. From September 2003 CREST introduced a new transaction to facilitate term repo settlement, known as 'RPO'. The RPO facility is available for all securities settled in CREST, including money market securities.[2]

The key features of the RPO service include:

- the ability for banks to select a basket of securities (up to ten different bonds) for each repo transacted;
- automatic creation of the closing leg (repurchase) instruction for the return of a security on maturity date;
- flexibility to substitute securities;
- facility to terminate specific lines in a repo trade and to roll-over current repo trades.

The advantage of RPO over DBV is that term repos can stay static, unless there is a need to terminate early or substitute securities, for the term of the trade. This obviates the need for large intra-day and daily cash and stock movements

CREST reference prices

After a repo trade has been agreed, the back offices of both parties will often use the CREST reference price (previously known as the CGO reference price or the gilt reference price) as the basis for settlement proceeds and other calculations.

---

[2] For further details see the relevant downloadable publications on *www.crestco.co.uk*

The CREST system uses data supplied by GEMMs for the calculation of reference prices. The reference prices for conventional gilt stocks are based on the clean mid-market closing (normally at 16 : 15 hours) prices supplied by members of the GEMM Association. These mid-prices are then adjusted to include accrued interest and quoted to five decimal places, expressed in £100 nominal of stock. Reference prices are updated daily.

Gilt strips trade on a yield basis. The reference price for strips is calculated from gross redemption yields using an 'actual/actual' formula – that is, compound interest for all strips divided by the actual number of days in the coupon period.

Delivery by value

DBV is a mechanism whereby a CREST member may borrow money from or lend money to another member against overnight gilt collateral. The CREST system automatically selects and delivers securities to a specified aggregate value on the basis of the previous night's reference prices; equivalent securities are returned the following business day. DBV functionality allows the giver and taker of collateral to specify the classes of security to be included within the DBV. The options are: all classes of security held within CREST, including strips and bulldogs; coupon bearing gilts and bulldogs; coupon bearing gilts and strips; only coupon bearing gilts.

DBV repo is a repo transaction in which the delivery of the securities is by the DBV mechanism in CREST; a series of DBV repos may be constructed to form an 'open' or 'term' DBV repo. DBV functionality allows repo interest to be automatically calculated and paid.

GILT REPO CODE OF BEST PRACTICE

The *Gilt Repo Code of Best Practice* sets out standards of best practice for gilt repo. It was introduced by the BoE in November 1995 ahead of the commencement of gilt repo trading in January 1996. The Code is set out in various sections, which we summarise below:

- *Preliminary issues* – market participants should ensure that they have adequate systems and controls for the business they intend to undertake. This includes internal controls, credit risk control systems, written procedures and systems for accounting and taxation.

- *Market professionals* – before dealing with a client for the first time, market professionals should either confirm that the client is already aware of the Code or draw it to the client's attention.
- *Legal agreement* – gilt repo transactions should be subject to a legal agreement between the two parties concerned. A market standard is the Gilt Repo Legal Agreement, and participants to gilt repo are strongly recommended to adopt this. This agreement is based on the BMA/ICMA GMRA (Section 8.1).
- *Margin* – participants in gilt repo should negotiate suitable initial margin reflecting both their assessment of their counterparty's creditworthiness and the market risks (e.g., duration of collateral) involved in the transaction. Participants should also monitor their net exposure to all counterparties on a daily basis.
- *Custody* – clients need to ensure that stock loan and repo transactions are identified accordingly to their custodian.
- *Default and close-out* – once the decision to default has been taken it is important that the process be carried out carefully. This includes the non-defaulting party doing everything in its power to ensure that default market values used in the close-out calculations are fair.

SELECTED REFERENCES

BoE (1995). *Gilt Repo Code of Best Practice*. Bank of England, November.
BoE (2003). *Quarterly Bulletin*, Spring, **43**(1), 16.
Choudhry, M. (2003). *The Gilt-edged Market*. Butterworth-Heinemann.

Chapter

6

....

OVERVIEW OF
REPO TRADING
AND THE
FUTURES CONTRACT
IMPLIED REPO RATE

The repo desk will have a central role on the trading floor, supporting the fixed-interest sales desk, hedging new issues, and working with the swaps and over-the-counter (OTC) options desks. In some banks and securities houses it will be placed within the Treasury or money market areas, whereas other firms will organise the repo desk as part of the bond operation. It is also not unusual to see equity repo carried out in a different area from bond repo.

In this chapter we introduce the approach to funding using repo. In the second part of the chapter we discuss the concept of the futures bond basis, which centres around the implied repo rate.

TRADING APPROACHES

Positive yield curve environment

When the yield curve is positively sloped, the conventional approach is to fund at the short end and lend at the long end of the curve. In essence, therefore, a bank would borrow, say, 1-week funds while simultaneously lending out at 2-week or 1-month. This is known as *funding short* and is illustrated at Figure 6.1.

A bank can effect the economic equivalent of borrowing at the short end of the yield curve and lending at the longer end through repo transactions, in our example a 1-week repo and a 6-month reverse repo. The bank then continuously rolls over its funding at 1-week intervals for the 6-month period. This is also known as *creating a tail*; here the 'tail' is the gap between 1 week and 6 months, the

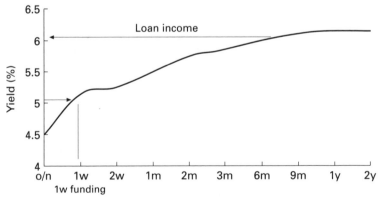

Figure 6.1 Positive yield curve – funding short.

interest rate 'gap' that the bank is exposed to. During the course of the trade, as the reverse repo has locked in a loan for 6 months, the bank is exposed to interest-rate risk should the slope or shape of the yield curve change. In this case – if short rates rise – the bank may see its profit margin shrink or turn into a funding loss.

As we see in Chapter 7, there is more than one explanation behind the shape of the yield curve at any particular time. A steeply positively shaped curve may indicate that the market expects interest rates to rise, although, as we have seen, this is also sometimes given as the reason for an inverted curve! However, generally speaking, trading volumes are higher in a positively sloping yield curve environment than those with a flat or negative shaped curve.

In a scenario of rising interest rates, it is advantageous to fund at the longer term, as part of overall asset–liability management (*ALM*). For instance, from June 2004 the US Federal Reserve began a cycle of interest-rate rises at a 'measured' pace of 25 basis points at each committee meeting. This took rates from a point of 1% in June 2004 to 4.25% in December 2005. During this time there was a consensus that these rises would take place, so market participants were not surprised each time rates were put up. In such an environment, it makes sense to fund at the longer term. Although market interest rates priced in successive rate rises, the forward curve often underplays what actual rates are at the future date. Hence, putting on longer term funding – say, 6 months or longer – was a safe and cost-saving strategy during this period.

Negative yield curve environment

In the case of an inverted yield curve, a bank will (all else being equal) lend at the short end of the curve and borrow at the longer end. This is known as *funding long* and is shown in Figure 6.2.

The example in Figure 6.2 shows a short cash position of 2-week maturity against a long cash position of 3-month maturity. The interest-rate *gap* of 10 weeks is the book's interest-rate exposure.

The inverted shape of the yield curve may indicate market expectations of a rise in short-term interest rates. Further along the yield curve the market may expect a benign inflationary environment, which is why the premium on longer term returns is lower than normal.

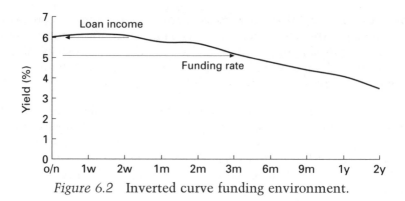

Figure 6.2   Inverted curve funding environment.

Yield curve arbitrage

This is a first principles type of *relative value* trading common on fixed-interest desks. If a trader believes that the shape of the yield curve is going to change, thus altering the yield *spread* between two bonds of differing maturities, she can position the book to benefit from such a move. A yield spread arbitrage trade is not market-directional – that is, it is not necessarily dependent on the direction that market moves in, but rather the change in the shape of the yield curve. As long as the trade is *duration-weighted* there is no first-order risk involved, although there is second-order risk in that if the shape of the yield curve changes in the opposite direction the trade will suffer a loss.

Consider the yield spread between 2-year and 5-year bonds; the trader believes that this spread will widen in the near future. The trade therefore looks like this:

- buy £x million of the 2-year bond;
- sell £y million of the 5-year bond, and borrow in the repo market.

The nominal amount of the 5-year bond will be a ratio of the respective *basis point values* multiplied by the amount of the 2-year bond. The trader will arrange the repo transaction simultaneously (or instruct the repo desk to do so). The funding for both bonds forms an important part of the rationale for the trade. As repo rates can be fixed for the anticipated term of the trade, the trader will know the net funding cost – irrespective of any change in market levels or yield spreads – and this cost is the break-even cost for the trade. A disciplined trader will have a time horizon for the trade, and the trade will be reviewed if the desired spread increase has not occurred by the

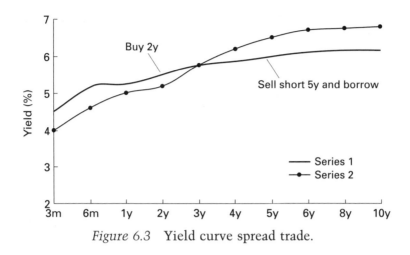

Figure 6.3 Yield curve spread trade.

expected time. In the case of the repo, however, the trader may wish to fix this at a shorter interval than the initial time horizon, and roll over as necessary.

Figure 6.3 illustrates the yield curve considerations involved.

'Series 1' represents the yield curve at the time the trade is put on, while 'Series 2' shows the curve at the point profit is taken and the trade is unwound. The increase in the 2-year versus 5-year spread is the profit made from the trade, minus the net funding.

Other spread trades

The trade described above is an example of relative value trading. There are many variations on this, including trades spanning different currencies and markets.

Example 6.1 Gilt-based spread.

The spread between 10-year UK gilts and 10-year German bunds has narrowed from a high of 160 basis points 6 months ago to a level of 91 basis points today. A trader feels that this spread will widen out again over the next 3 weeks. The trader therefore sells the gilt and buys the bunds in anticipation of this move. Both trades are funded/covered in the respective repo markets. This trade also requires the trader to have a view on the sterling/euro exchange rate, as any profit from the trade could be reduced or eliminated by adverse movements in the exchange rate. Figure 6.4 illustrates the starting point for the trade.

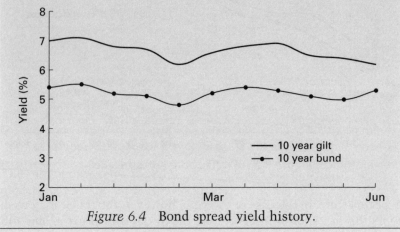

Figure 6.4   Bond spread yield history.

SPECIALS TRADING

The existence of a repo market allows the demand to borrow and lend stocks to be cleared by the price mechanism (and more efficiently than in traditional stock lending). It is to be expected that when specific stocks are in demand, for one of a number of reasons, the premium on obtaining them rises. Factors contributing to demand for *specials* include the following:

- *government bond auctions* – the bond to be issued is shorted by market makers in anticipation of a new supply of stock and due to client demand;
- *outright short selling* – whether deliberate position-taking on the trader's view, or market makers selling stock on client demand;
- *hedging* – including bond underwriters who will short the benchmark government bond that the corporate bond is priced against;
- *derivatives-trading* – such as basis ('cash-and-carry') trading creating demand for a specific stock.

Natural holders of government bonds can benefit from issues *going special*, which is when the demand for specific stocks is such that the rate for borrowing them is reduced. The lower repo rate reflects

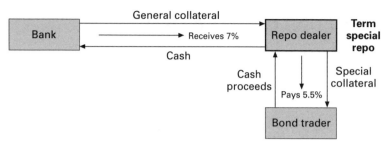

Figure 6.5   Specials trading.

the premium for borrowing the stock. Note that the party borrowing the special stock is lending cash; it is the rate payable on the cash that he has lent that is depressed.

The holder of a stock that has gone special can obtain cheap funding for the issue itself, by lending it out. Alternatively, the holder can lend the stock and obtain cash in exchange in a repo, for which the rate payable is lower than the interbank rate. These funds can then be lent out as either secured funding (in a repo) or as unsecured funding, enabling the specials holder to lock in a profit. For example, a repo dealer holds an issue trading at 5.5% in the 1-week. The equivalent GC rate is 7%. By lending the stock out the dealer can lock in the profit by on-lending 1-week cash at 7%, or at a higher rate in the interbank market. This is illustrated in Figure 6.5.[1]

There is a positive correlation between changes in a stock that trades expensive to the yield curve and changes in the degree to which it trades special. Theory would predict this, since traders will maintain short positions for bonds with high funding (repo) costs only if the anticipated fall in the price of the bond is large enough to cover this funding premium. When stock is perceived as being expensive – for example, after an auction announcement – this creates a demand for short positions and, hence, greater demand for the paper in repo. At other times the stock may go tight in the repo market, following which it will tend to be bid higher in the *cash* market as traders close out existing shorts (which have become expensive to finance). At the same time, traders and investors may attempt to buy the stock outright since it will now be cheap to finance in repo. The link between dearness in the cash market and special status in the repo market flows both ways.

---

[1] A spread of 150 bps below GC is very special indeed!

CREDIT INTERMEDIATION

The government bond market will trade at a lower rate than other money market instruments, reflecting its status as the best credit. This allows the spreads between markets of different credits to be exploited. The following are examples of credit intermediation trades:

- a repo dealer lends general collateral (GC) currently trading at Libor-25, and uses the cash to buy certificates of deposit (CDs) trading at Libor-12.5;
- a repo dealer borrows specific collateral in the stock lending market, pays a fee and on-lends the stock in the repo market at the GC rate; the cash is then lent in the interbank market at a higher rate;
- a repo dealer trades repo in the GC market, and using this cash reverses in emerging market collateral at a spread, say, 400 basis points higher.

MATCHED BOOK TRADING

The growth of repo markets has led to repo match book trading desks. Essentially, this is market-making in repo; dealers make two-way trading prices in various securities, irrespective of their underlying positions. In fact, the term 'matched book' is a misnomer; most matched books are deliberately mismatched as part of a view on the short-term yield curve. Traders put on positions to take advantage of (i) short-term interest-rate movements and (ii) anticipated supply and demand in the underlying stock. Many of the trading ideas and strategies described in this book are examples of match book trading.

Matched book trading can involve the following types of trades:

- *taking a view on interest rates* – for example, the dealer bids for 1-month GC and offers 3-month GC, expecting the yield curve to invert;
- *taking a view on specials* – for example, the trader borrows stock in the stock lending market for use in repo once (as the trader expects) it goes *special*;
- *credit intermediation* – for example, a dealer reverses in Brady bonds from a Latin American bank, at a rate of Libor +200 and

offers this stock to a US money market investor at a rate of Libor
+20.

Principals and principal intermediaries with large volumes of repos
and reverse repos, such as the market makers mentioned above, are
said to be running 'matched books'. An undertaking to provide two-
way prices is made to provide customers with a continuous financing
service for long and short positions and also as part of proprietary
trading. Traders will mismatch positions in order to take advantage
of a combination of two factors, which are short-term interest-rate
movements and anticipated supply/demand in the underlying bond.

Example 6.2   Matched book trade.

ABC Bank reverses in gilts/other collateral for 3 months at 6.25%
and repoes out gilts/other collateral for 2 months at 6.00%.

ABC Bank has therefore lent cash for 3 months at 6.25% and,
simultaneously, borrowed cash for 2 months at 6%. The mismatch
exposure in the 2–3 month period is the tail. In this case the break-
even on the tail of the trade is 6.75%. ABC has locked in a 25-bps
profit for 2 months; therefore, it would have to lose 50 basis points
or more in the last month in order to lose money on the trade. This
might happen if interest rates were to rise significantly, forcing the
Bank to fund the exposure at a higher rate.

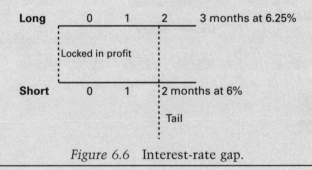

Figure 6.6   Interest-rate gap.

HEDGING TOOLS

For dealers who are not looking to trade around term mismatch or
other spreads, there is more than one way to hedge the repo trade.
The best hedge for any trade is an exact offsetting trade. This is not

always possible, nor indeed always desirable, as it may reduce profit. However, a similar offsetting trade will limit *basis risk*. The residual risk will be that between, say, GC and special or interest-rate gap risk.

Futures strip

A forward term interest-rate gap exposure can be hedged using interest-rate futures. In the sterling market the instrument will typically be the 90-day short sterling future traded on LIFFE. A strip of futures can be used to hedge the term gap. The trader buys futures contracts to the value of the exposure and for the term of the gap. Any change in cash rates should be hedged by the offsetting move in futures prices.

Figure 6.7 shows Bloomberg screen TED and the hedge strip for a short-dated gilt, the $7\frac{1}{2}\%$ Treasury 2006. It shows the contracts that must be sold to hedge a holding of nominal GBP 10 million of this bond, as at 28 December 2005. The 'stub' number of contracts would, in practice, be added to the front month; so, the futures strip for this

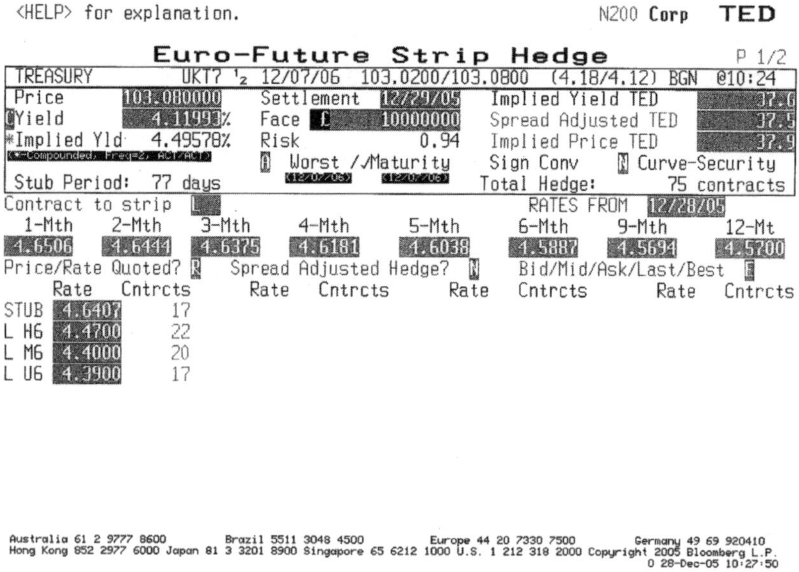

Figure 6.7 Bloomberg screen TED, futures hedge strip for holding of short-dated gilt, 28 December 2005.

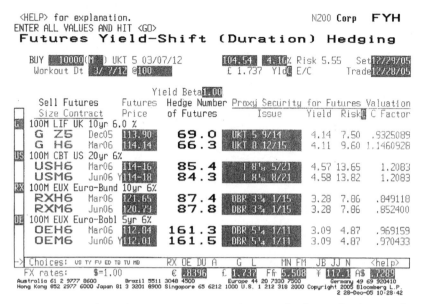

Figure 6.8   Bloomberg screen FYH, futures hedge calculation for holding of long-dated gilt, 28 December 2005.

© Bloomberg L.P. Used with permission. Visit *www.bloomberg.com*

position would look like 30 lots of the March 2006 short sterling contract, 20 of the June 2006 and 17 lots of the September 2006 future.

Figure 6.8 shows screen FYH which is the screen used to calculate the hedge for a long-dated bond, in this case GBP 10 million of the 5% Treasury 2012 gilt, as at the same date. We see that the hedge is 69 lots of the December 2005 long gilt future and 67 of the March 2006.[2]

Forward rate agreements

Forward rate agreements (*FRAs*) are similar in concept to interest-rate futures and are also off-balance sheet instruments. Under a FRA

---

[2] This screen was printed on 28 December 2005. The author was surprised to see the December 2005 contract make an appearance, as it would long since have ceased to be the 'front month' contract. In practice, we would hedge this position on this date with the March 2006 and June 2006 contracts.

a buyer agrees notionally to borrow and a seller to lend a specified notional amount at a fixed rate for a specified period, the contract to commence on an agreed date in the future. On this date (the 'fixing date') the actual rate is taken and, according to its position versus the original trade rate, the borrower or lender will receive an interest payment on the notional sum equal to the difference between the trade rate and the actual rate. The sum paid over is present-valued as it is transferred at the start of the notional loan period, whereas in a cash market trade interest would be handed over at the end of the loan period. As FRAs are off-balance sheet contracts no actual borrowing or lending of cash takes place; hence, the use of the term 'notional'. In hedging an interest-rate gap in the cash period, the trader will buy a FRA contract that equates to the term gap for a nominal amount equal to his exposure in the cash market. Should rates move against him in the cash market, the gain on the FRA should (in theory) compensate for the loss in the cash trade.

Interest-rate swaps

An interest-rate swap is an off-balance sheet agreement between two parties to make periodic interest payments to the other. Payments are on a predetermined set of dates in the future, based on a notional principal amount; one party is the *fixed rate payer*, the rate agreed at the start of the swap, and the other party is the *floating-rate payer*, the floating rate being determined during the life of the swap by reference to a specific market rate or index. There is no exchange of principal, only of the interest payments on this principal amount. Note that our description is for a plain vanilla swap contract; it is common to have variations on this theme – for instance, *floating–floating* swaps where both payments are floating rate, as well as *cross-currency* swaps where there is an exchange of an equal amount of different currencies at the start and end dates for the swap.

An interest-rate swap can be used to hedge the fixed-rate risk arising from the purchase of a bond during a repo arbitrage or spread trade. The terms of the swap should match the payment dates and maturity date of the bond. The idea is to match the cash flows from the bond with equal and opposite payments in the swap contract, which will hedge the bond position. For example, if a trader has purchased a bond, he will be receiving fixed-rate coupon payments on the nominal value of the bond. To hedge this position the trader buys a swap contract for the same nominal value in which he will be paying the same fixed-rate payment; the net cash flow is a receipt of floating interest-rate payments. A bond issuer, on the other hand, may issue bonds of a particular type because of investor demand for such paper, but prefer to have the interest exposure on his debt in some other form. So, for example, a UK company issues fixed-rate bonds denominated in, say, Australian dollars, swaps the proceeds into sterling and pays floating-rate interest on the sterling amount. As part of the swap he will be receiving fixed-rate Australian dollars which neutralises the exposure arising from the bond issue. At the termination of the swap (which must coincide with the maturity of the bond) the original currency amounts are exchanged back, enabling the issuer to redeem the holders of the bond in Australian dollars.

THE IMPLIED REPO RATE AND BASIS TRADING

Basis trading, also known as *cash-and-carry* trading, refers to the activity of simultaneously trading cash bonds and the related bond futures contract. An open repo market is essential for the smooth operation of basis trading. Most futures exchanges offer at least one bond futures contract. Major exchanges, such as CBOT, offer contracts along the entire yield curve; others, such as LIFFE, provide a market in contracts on bonds denominated in a range of major currencies.

Contract definition

Bond futures, like commodity futures, are based on the delivery of a tangible asset – a particular bond – at some date in the future. As an example, the LIFFE long gilt contract, one of the most active financial futures contracts, is described in Figure 6.9, which is Bloomberg page DES for this contract.

Note the contract specifications: any gilt with a term to maturity of between $8\frac{3}{4}$ and 13 years at time of contract expiry is eligible for delivery into the contract. The notional coupon of the bond represented by the contract is 6%, which was changed from 7% from the March 2004 contract onwards.

So, the definition of the gilt contract detailed in Figure 6.9 calls for the delivery of a UK gilt with an effective maturity of between $8\frac{3}{4}$ to

G A Comdty DES   N200 Comdty **DES**
Type # <GO> For Related Function
   Futures Contract Description   Page 1/2

Exchange (LIF) LIFFE		Related Functions	
Name	LONG GILT FUTURE Mar06	1) CT	Contract Table
Ticker	G H6 <CMDTY>	2) FHG	Futures History Graph
Notional	UK 10yr 6.0 %	3) EXS	Expiration Schedule
Contract Size	GBP 100,000	4) DLV	Cheapest to Deliver
Value of 1.0 pt	£ 1,000	5) WECO	World Economic Releases
Tick Size	.01	Margin Limits	
Tick Value	£ 10		Speculator
Current Price	114.14	Initial	1210
Contract Value	£ 114,140 @ 10:27:22		
Cycle --- --- Mar --- --- Jun --- --- Sep --- --- Dec			

Trading Hours		Gilt issues having maturity of 8 ¾ to 13 years
London	Local	from the 1st calendar day of the delivery month.
08:00-18:00	08:00-18:00	Contract launched on LIFFE CONNECT April 12, 1999.
		On last Trade date Trading ends at 11am London
		time **Starting with the March 04' contract the
		underlying notional changed from 7% to 6%**

First Delivery	Wed Mar 1, 2006	Life High 114.36	Generics Available
Last Delivery	Fri Mar 31, 2006	Life Low 109.29	
Last Trade	Wed Mar 29, 2006		G 1 <CMDTY>
First Notice	Mon Feb 27, 2006		G 2 <CMDTY>
First Trade	Wed Mar 30, 2005		G 3 <CMDTY>

Australia 61 2 9777 8600   Brazil 5511 3048 4500   Europe 44 20 7330 7500   Germany 49 69 920410
Hong Kong 852 2977 6000 Japan 81 3 3201 8900 Singapore 65 6212 1000 U.S. 1 212 318 2000 Copyright 2005 Bloomberg L.P.
                                                                                      0 28-Dec-05 10:28:55

Figure 6.9   Bloomberg page DES showing long gilt futures contract specification.

© Bloomberg L.P. Used with permission. Visit *www.bloomberg.com*

13 years and a 6% coupon. Of course, there would be problems if the definition of deliverable bonds were restricted solely to those with a coupon of exactly 6%. At times, there may be no bonds having this precise coupon. Where there was one or more such bonds, the size of the futures market in relation to the size of the bond issue would expose the market to price manipulation. To avoid this, futures exchanges design contracts in such a way as to prevent anyone cornering the market. In the case of the long gilt and most similar contracts this is achieved by allowing the delivery of *any* bond with a sufficient maturity. Note that the holder of a long position in futures would prefer to receive a high-coupon bond with significant accrued interest, while those short of the future would favour delivering a cheaper low-coupon bond shortly after the coupon date. This conflict of interest is resolved by adjusting the *invoice amount* – the amount paid in exchange for the bond – to account for coupon rate and timing of the bond actually delivered.

Equation (6.1) defines this invoice amount:

$$\text{Inv}_{\text{amt}} = P_{\text{fut}} \times CF + AI \qquad (6.1)$$

where Inv_{amt} = Invoice amount;
        P_{fut} = Futures price;
        CF = Conversion factor;
        AI = Accrued interest.

Every bond deliverable under a particular futures contract, said to be in the *delivery basket*, will have its own *conversion factor* or *price factor*, which is intended to compensate for the coupon and timing differences of deliverable bonds. The exchange publishes tables of conversion factors in advance of a contract starting to trade, and these remain fixed for the life of the contract. These numbers will be smaller than 1.0 for bonds having coupons less than 7%, and greater than 1.0, otherwise.

Box 6.1   Conversion factor.

The conversion factor gives the price of an individual cash bond such that its yield to maturity on the delivery day of the futures contract is equal to the notional coupon of the contract. The product of the conversion factor and the futures price is the forward price available in the futures market for that cash bond (plus the cost of funding, referred to as the gross basis). If the coupon of the bond is above the notional coupon, its conversion factor will be greater than 1. If its coupon is below the notional coupon, its conversion factor will be less than 1.

See Appendix B.

As an illustration Figure 6.10 lists the sets of conversion factors calculated by LIFFE for gilts deliverable into the March 2006 long gilt futures contract, as listed on page 'DLV' of a Bloomberg terminal on 28 December 2005.

Page DLV on Bloomberg will list deliverable bonds for any selected futures contract. Bonds are listed in order of declining *implied repo rate*; the user can select in increasing or decreasing order of implied repo rate, basis, yield, maturity, coupon or duration. The user can also select the price source for the bonds (in our example set at 'Bloomberg Generic' rather than any specific bank or market maker) and the current cash repo rate.

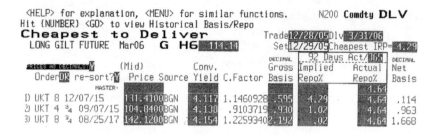

Figure 6.10 Bloomberg page DLV for March 2006 long gilt contract, showing conversion factors for deliverable gilts.

© Bloomberg L.P. Used with permission. Visit *www.bloomberg.com*

Conversion factors

A particular bond that remains in the basket over a length of time will have different conversion factors for successive contracts. For example, the 8% Treasury maturing on 7 December 2015, which was the cheapest-to-deliver (*CTD*) gilt for the March 2006 contract, had the following conversion factors per successive contract:[3]

December 2004	1.159 5576
March 2005	1.156 8327
June 2005	1.154 3448
September 2005	1.151 4966
December 2005	1.148 9734
March 2006	1.143 0928

Note how the conversion factor moves towards 1 for each successive contract.

---

[2] *Source*: Bloomberg L.P.

The yield obtainable on bonds with differing coupons but identical maturities can be equalised by adjusting the price for each. This principle is used to calculate the conversion factors for different bonds. The conversion factor for each bond is the price per £1 (or per $1, EUR 1, etc.) such that every bond would provide an investor with the same yield if purchased. The yield selected for the calculations is the same as the coupon rate in the definition of the futures contract, 6% in the case of the long gilt contract traded on LIFFE.

Other things being equal, bonds with a higher coupon will have larger conversion factors than those with lower coupons. For bonds with the same coupon, maturity has an influence, though this is slightly less obvious. For bonds with coupons below the notional rate defined in the contract description, the conversion factor is smaller for bonds with a longer maturity. The opposite is true for bonds carrying coupons in excess of the notional coupon rate, for which the conversion factor will be larger the longer the maturity. This effect arises from the mathematics of fixed-interest securities. Bonds with coupon below current market yields will trade at a 'discount' (i.e., below par). This discount is larger the longer the maturity, because it is a disadvantage to hold a bond paying a coupon lower than current market rates, and this disadvantage is greater the longer the period to the bond maturing. Conversely, bonds with coupons above current market yields trade at a premium (i.e., above par), which will be greater the longer the maturity.

Most futures exchanges calculate conversion factors effective for either the exact delivery date, where a single date is defined, or (as at LIFFE) for the first day of the delivery month if delivery can take place at any time during the delivery month.

The cheapest-to-deliver bond

Using *conversion factors* provides an effective system for making all deliverable bonds perfect substitutes for one another. The system is not perfect, however. Conversion factors are calculated to equalise returns at a single uniform yield, the notional coupon rate specified in the contract specification. In practice though, bonds trade at different yields, resulting in the concept of the yield curve as described in Chapter 7. Hence, despite the use of conversion factors, bonds will not be precisely 'equal' at the time of delivery. Some bonds will be relatively more expensive, some cheaper; one particular bond will be the *cheapest-to-deliver* bond. The CTD bond is an important concept in the pricing of bond futures contracts.

Determining the CTD bond

To determine which bond is the CTD, consider the following trading strategy executed during a delivery month:

- buy £100,000 nominal of a deliverable bond;
- sell one futures contract;
- immediately initiate the delivery process.

The amount paid for the bond will be the market price plus accrued interest:

$$P_{con} = P_{bond} + AI \tag{6.2}$$

where P_{con} = Total consideration paid for the bond;
            P_{bond} = Market price for the bond;
            AI = Accrued interest.

The invoice amount Inv_{amt} received when delivering the bond against the short futures position has already been defined in Equation (6.1). The resultant profit from the trading strategy is then:

$$P_{profit} = Inv_{amt} - P_{con}$$
$$= (P_{fut} \times CF + AI) - (P_{bond} + AI)$$
$$= (P_{fut} \times CF - P_{bond}) \tag{6.3}$$

The bond for which this expression is maximised will be the CTD bond during the delivery month. A more complex formula can be derived to determine the CTD bond prior to the delivery month, taking into account *carrying* costs.

The gross basis

The previous section introduced the concept of the *gross basis*. Basis trading arises from the difference between the current clean price of a bond and the clean price at which the bond is bought through the purchase of a futures contract. The difference between these two prices is known as the 'gross basis'.

The formula for calculating the gross basis is therefore:

$$Basis = P_{bond} - (P_{fut} \times CF_{bond}) \tag{6.4}$$

The gross basis can be explained essentially as the difference between the running yield on the bond and the current repo (money market) rate. However, a residual factor is due to the delivery option implicit in the design of the futures contract and to the daily marking-to-market of the contract, both of which are more difficult to quantify. This residual amount is known as the *net basis*. The bond with the lowest net basis will be the CTD bond. Net basis is the gross basis adjusted for net carry. Net carry is the actual coupon income and re-investment less borrowing expense, which is at the security's actual repo (money market) rate. The net basis is therefore the true 'economic basis'. A positive value represents a *loss* or net cost to the long cash/short futures position, and the net basis is the expected *profit* for the short cash/long futures position (where actual repo is the reverse repo rate). The opposite is true for negative net basis values.

Traders take a view on the size of the gross basis and trade according to their view.

Real world trading and reverse cash-and-carry strategy

Generally, all bonds on all exchanges will produce a negative result for the strategy of buying the bond and simultaneously selling the futures, and initiating the delivery process. Bid–offer price spreads will also erode a theoretical advantage. This implies that the opposite strategy, buying the futures and selling the bond – known as *reverse cash-and-carry* – would lead to a profit. In theory, the trader can earn the repo rate on short-sale proceeds; such a trade is indicated when the implied repo rate is lower than the actual repo rate. However, the party who is short futures always initiates the delivery process and chooses, among other things, which bond to deliver. A trader tempted to execute a reverse cash-and-carry by shorting the $8\frac{3}{4}\%$ Treasury 2017 in a bid to secure a 2.192 basis points riskless profit (see Figure 6.10) should note that the short future is most unlikely to deliver that particular bond. A reverse cash-and-carry trade in the CTD bond may also come unstuck if changing market circumstances result in the bond losing its status as the CTD bond.

The delivery date of the bonds is at the option of the short future, and will depend on the yield of the bond; if the yield is higher than the money market (repo) rate, the bond will be delivered at the end of the month, while if the yield is lower than the money market rate, delivery will be on the first day of the delivery month. Although delivery is at the short future's option and can be at any time during the delivery month, in practice the short will always deliver on one of the two dates noted above, for if the yield is higher than the money market rate the bondholder will earn the higher return until the last possible moment, whereas if the yield on the bond is lower than the money market rate delivery will take place as soon as possible.

In addition to choosing the bond to deliver, the short futures trader can also exploit other futures inherent in the delivery process which can result in a slight advantage over the party who is long futures. This is outside the scope of this book and the interested reader should consult other texts, including those listed at the end of the chapter.

The implied repo rate

We have stated that exchange-traded bond futures, such as LIFFE's long gilt contract, require physical delivery of a real bond. For the gilt contract this will be any eligible gilt with a maturity of $8\frac{3}{4}$ to 13 years. However, only the bond that is the CTD, from the point of view of the short futures holder, will be delivered.

The CTD gilt can be delivered on any business day of the delivery month, but in practice only 2 days are ever used. If the current yield on the CTD gilt exceeds the money market interest rate, the bond will be delivered on the last business day of the month, because the short earns more by holding on to the bond than by delivering it and investing the proceeds in the money market; otherwise, the bond will be delivered on the first business day of the delivery month.

Until very recently, a gilt that was trading *special ex-dividend* on the proposed delivery day was not eligible for delivery. However, from August 1998 the provision for special ex-dividend trading was removed from gilts, so this consideration no longer applies. Other gilts that are not eligible are index-linked, partly paid or convertible bonds.

Invoice amount

When the bond is delivered, the long pays the short an invoice amount:

$$\text{Inv}_{\text{amt}} = \left[\frac{\text{Settlement price}}{100} \times CF \times \text{Nominal value of gilt}\right] + AI \quad (6.5)$$

The settlement price – or *exchange delivery settlement price* (*EDSP*) – is the trading price per £100 nominal for the futures contract on the last day of trading, and is confirmed by the exchange. The invoice amount includes accrued interest because the futures contract is traded at a clean price and does not include accrued interest. Gilts trade at a *clean* price but have accrued interest added on (called *dirty* price).

We have stated that the conversion factor (or price factor) determines the appropriate price of the bond that is delivered. It is calculated as being the price per £1 nominal at which the bond delivered has a yield to maturity of 6%.

Calculating the implied repo rate

Another way of looking at the concept of the CTD bond is in terms of the *implied repo rate*. The CTD bond is the bond that gives the highest implied repo rate (*IRR*) to the short from a cash-and-carry trade – that is, the strategy of buying the bond (with borrowed funds) in the cash market and selling it in the futures market.

To illustrate, we can calculate the IRR for the 9% Treasury 2008, assumed to be currently trading at 129.0834. Assume also that the December 1998 long gilt futures contract is trading at 114.50. The date is 1 October. The money market rate on this date is 7.25%. As the current (or *running*) yield on the 9% 2008, at 6.972%, is lower than the money market rate, it will be delivered at the beginning of December (i.e., in 61 days from now). To identify the CTD bond we would need to calculate the IRR for all eligible bonds. We will use conversion factors calculated and given out by LIFFE before the futures contract began trading.

Consider the 9% 2008. The cash outflow in a cash-and-carry trade is as follows:

Dirty price of bond	129.0834
plus Interest cost (1 Oct–1 Dec)	$129.0834 \times \left[0.0725 \left(\frac{61}{365} \right) \right]$
equals	130.6474

The bond (whose price includes 171 days interest on 1 October) has to be financed at the money market rate of 7.25% for the 61 days between 1 October and 1 December, when the bond (if it happens to be the CTD) is delivered into the futures market.

The cash inflow per £100 nominal as a result of this trade is:

Implied clean price of bond (1 Dec)	114.50
plus Futures price (1 Oct) × Conversion factor	114.50 × 1.140 7155
plus Accrued interest (1 Oct–1 Dec)	$£9 \times \left(\dfrac{61}{365} \right)$
equals	132.116 03

The implied price of the bond on 1 December equals the futures price on 1 October multiplied by the conversion factor for the bond. Because the futures price is quoted clean, accrued interest has to be added to obtain the implied dirty price on 1 December.

This cash-and-carry trade which operates for 61 days from 1 October to 1 December generates a rate of return or *implied repo rate* of:

$$\text{Implied repo rate} = \left(\frac{132.11603 - 130.6474}{130.6474} \right) \times \frac{365}{61} \times 100 = 6.726\%$$

The rate implied by a cash-and-carry strategy is known as a repo rate because it is equivalent to a *repurchase* agreement with the futures market. In effect, the short lends money to the futures market: the short agrees to buy a bond with a simultaneous provision to sell it back to the market at a predetermined price and to receive a rate of interest on his money, the repo rate.

The IRR for all deliverable bonds can be calculated in this way. The only modification required is if a bond goes ex-dividend between trade date and delivery date, in which case the interest accrued is negative during the ex-dividend period. Nowadays, it is more usual to calculate IRRs and net basis figures from an off-the-shelf spreadsheet program or an external source such as Bloomberg.

Example 6.3   Calculating the gross and net basis.

This example calculation relates to the gilt contract before the recent changes; therefore, the notional coupon is 10% and pricing is in 32nds ('ticks'). The 'special ex' rule also applies:

June long gilt future	109-21/32
CTD bond (8½% 2007)	106-11/32

Conversion factor $(8\frac{1}{2}\%\ 2007)$ 0.967 4064
Repo rate   6.36%

The clean price at which a bond is bought through use of a futures contract is:

Futures price × Conversion factor

Therefore, the cost of buying the $8\frac{1}{2}\%$ 2007 through the futures contract is:

$$\frac{109\text{-}21}{32} \times 0.967\ 4064 = 106.082\ 16$$

The market price is 106-11/32; therefore, the gross basis is:

$$\frac{106\text{-}11}{32} - 106.082\ 16 = 0.261\ 59$$

Due to the special ex rule in this case, the last day for delivery of $8\frac{1}{2}\%$ 2007 into the futures contract is 12 June. Assume the bond is purchased in the market on 24 April, for settlement on 25 April. The total price paid including accrued interest will be 108.649 23. To finance that using repo for 48 days until 12 June will cost £0.908 7243. The holder of the gilt will however earn 48 days' accrued interest of £1.117 8082. Therefore, buying the bond direct gives the owner an income advantage of £0.209 0839.

The difference between the gross basis and this income advantage is £0.216 159 − £0.209 0839 (i.e., £0.0525). It therefore represents the gain by buying the gilt using the futures contract rather than buying directly in the market.

Of course, the long gilt contract gives the futures seller the right to deliver any of the gilts in the delivery basket and on any day of the delivery month. If the CTD is bought through a futures contract the buyer may find that, because of market movements, a different gilt is delivered. The futures short in effect holds an option which decreases the value of the futures contract to the long.

For this reason the *net* basis is usually positive. The futures contract is also marked-to-market which means that the gain or loss on the contract is spread over the life of the contract, in contrast to a forward contract. This effect is small but will again lead to the net basis differing from 0.

For theoretical background to basis trading and the debate on net basis versus implied repo rates see Appendix B.

Hedging implications

The behaviour of the bond futures contract and the CTD bond are closely linked. For this reason the futures contract can be used to hedge a portfolio of bonds. This is illustrated in the following examples for the US Treasury futures contract, which has a size of $100,000.

CTD bond	10.375% 2006
Conversion factor	1.15000

Example 6.4

Hedge $10 million CTD bonds

$$= \frac{10,000,000}{100,000} \times 1.150\,00$$

$$= 115 \text{ contracts}$$

Example 6.5

Hedge portfolio of $10 million US Treasury bonds, with price volatility of half that of the CTD bond

$$= \frac{10,000,000}{100,000} \times 1.150\,00 \times 0.5$$

$$= 58 \text{ contracts}$$

The hedge quantity is therefore:

$$\frac{\text{Nominal size of portfolio}}{\text{Contract size}} \times \text{CTD conversion factor}$$

$$\times \frac{\text{Basis point value of portfolio}}{\text{Basis point value CTD}}$$

Example 6.6   Hedging calculation.

Settlement date   5 February 1994

A fixed income fund currently holds EUR 50 million of 7% bunds maturing on 24 September 2014. The Bundesbank has announced a new issue of a 10-year bund; the fund manager is concerned that this additional supply may depress the market. Therefore, on 5 February – 2 days before the auction – the fund manager puts on a futures hedge. On that day the March bund futures contract on LIFFE is trading at 84.05. Note also the following:

	CTD bund	Portfolio 7% bund
Price	86.35	91.86
Yield	8.33%	7.80%
Duration	7.8 years	10.8 years
Conversion factor	1.028 811	1.115 887

LIFFE's bund contract is for EUR 250,000 of a bund with notional coupon of 6%. Prices are quoted in hundredths, tick value is EUR 25. Accrued interest is quoted on a 30/360 day basis.

The formula for modified duration is:

$$\frac{\text{Duration}}{1 + \text{Yield}}$$

(a) How many futures contracts are required to hedge a EUR 50 million position in the CTD bond?

$$\frac{50,000,000}{250,000} \times 1.028\,811 = 206 \text{ contracts}$$

(rounded to whole numbers).

(b) Calculate the adjusted hedge amount from that in (a) to allow for the different duration of the EUR 50 million bond held in the portfolio:

(i) BPV_{ctd} $\quad = \dfrac{\text{Modified duration}}{100} \times \dfrac{\text{Dirty price}}{100}$

$\qquad\qquad = 0.063$

(ii) BPVPort $\quad = 0.095$

Number of futures contracts to hedge:

$$\frac{50,000,000}{250,000} \times 1.028\,811 \times \frac{0.095}{0.063} = 310$$

Example 6.7

On 8 February after the auction the fund manager unwinds the hedge by closing the futures position at 83.82. On that day the 7% Bund trades at 91.56:

(a) Profit/Loss on futures position $= 23 \times 25 \times 310$

$= $ DEM 178,250

Profit/Loss on cash position $= 0.30 \times \dfrac{50,000,000}{100}$

$= (150,000)$

Net profit $= $ DEM 28,250

Note this ignores funding costs and accrued interest in the calculation.

(b) What is the gross basis between the cash position and the futures price at the time the hedge was put on and at the time it was unwound?

$$\text{Gross basis} = \text{Bond price} - \frac{\text{Futures}}{\text{price}} \times \frac{\text{Bond's conversion}}{\text{factor}}$$

Before: $91.86 - (84.05 \times 1.116) = -1.9398$
After: $91.56 - (83.82 - 1.116) = -1.9831$

(c) What does the change in the gross basis suggest?

The basis has increased between the time the hedge was put on and then unwound. This would indicate a greater cost of carry now associated with the bond.

SELECTED REFERENCES

Choudhry, M. (2006). *The Futures Bond Basis* (2nd edn). John Wiley & Sons.

Fabozzi, F. (1988). *Fixed Income Mathematics*. Probus Publishing.

Fabozzi, F. (2005). *The Handbook of Fixed Income Securities* (5th edn). Dow Jones/Irwin.

Kolb, R., *Futures, Options and Swaps*, 3rd edition, Blackwell 2000.

Chapter

7

....

REPO AND
THE YIELD CURVE

In Chapter 6 we discussed how the shape of the curve and interest-rate expectations drive the funding decision. In this chapter we present further essential background information on zero-coupon (spot) and forward interest rates. Repo market participants should be aware of the concepts discussed in this chapter.

ZERO-COUPON RATES

Zero (or spot), par and forward rates are closely linked. This section will explain and derive the different interest rates and explain their application in the markets.

The term 'zero-coupon' originates from the bond market and describes a bond which has no coupons. The yield on a zero-coupon bond can be viewed as a true yield, if the paper is held to maturity as no re-investment is involved and there are no interim cash flows vulnerable to a change in interest rates. Note the following:

- a set of zero-coupon rates exists for every major currency;
- zero-coupon rates can be used to value any future cash flow.

Where zero-coupon bonds are traded the yield on a zero-coupon bond of a particular maturity is the zero-coupon rate for that maturity. However, it is not necessary to have zero-coupon bonds in order to deduce zero-coupon rates. It is possible to calculate zero-coupon rates from a range of market rates and prices, including coupon bonds, interest-rate futures and currency deposit. The price of a zero-coupon bond of a particular maturity defines directly the value today of a cash flow due on the bond's redemption date, and indirectly the zero-coupon rate for that maturity. For example, if a 5-year zero-coupon bond is priced at 60, the present value of any other cash flow due on the same date is also 60% of its future value. Similarly, a cash flow of 30 due in 5 years would be worth $30 \times 0.60 = 18$ today.

DISCOUNT FACTORS AND THE DISCOUNT FUNCTION

It is possible to determine a set of discount factors from market rates. A discount factor is a number in the range 0 to 1 which can be used to obtain the present value of some future value:

$$PV_t = v_t \times FV_t \qquad (7.1)$$

where PV_t = Present value of the future cash flow occurring at time t;
          FV_t = Future cash flow occurring at time t;
          v_t = Discount factor for cash flows occurring at time t.

Discount factors can be calculated most easily from zero-coupon rates; Equations (7.2) and (7.3) apply to zero-coupon rates for periods up to 1 year and over 1 year, respectively:

$$Df_t = \frac{1}{(1 + z_t T_t)} \qquad (7.2)$$

$$Df_t = \frac{1}{(1 + z_t)^{T_t}} \qquad (7.3)$$

where Df_t = Discount factor for cash flows occurring at time t;
          z_t = Zero-coupon rate for the period to time t;
          T_t = Time from the value date to time t, expressed in years and fractions of a year.

Individual zero-coupon rates allow discount factors to be calculated at specific points along the maturity spectrum. As cash flows may occur at any time in the future, and not necessarily at convenient times like in 3 months or 1 year, discount factors often need to be calculated for every possible date in the future. The complete set of discount factors is called the *discount function*.

SPOT AND FORWARD RATES: BOOT-STRAPPING FROM THE PAR YIELD CURVE

Spot rates and boot-strapping

Par, spot and forward rates have a close mathematical relationship. Here we explain and derive these different interest rates and explain their application in the markets. Note that *spot* interest rates are also called *zero-coupon* rates, because they are the interest rates that would be applicable to a zero-coupon bond. The two terms are used synonymously; however, strictly speaking they are not exactly similar. Zero-coupon bonds are actual market instruments, and the yield on zero-coupon bonds can be observed in the market. A spot rate is a purely theoretical construct, and so cannot actually be observed directly. For our purposes though, we will use the terms synonymously.

A *par yield* is the yield to maturity on a bond that is trading at par. This means that the yield is equal to the bond's coupon level. A zero-coupon bond is a bond which has no coupons, and therefore only one cash flow, the redemption payment on maturity. It is therefore a *discount* instrument, as it is issued at a discount to par and redeemed at par. The yield on a zero-coupon bond can be viewed as a true yield at the time that it is purchased, if the paper is held to maturity. This is because no re-investment of coupons is involved and, hence, there are no interim cash flows vulnerable to a change in interest rates. Zero-coupon yields are the key determinant of value in the capital markets, and they are calculated and quoted for every major currency. Zero-coupon rates can be used to value any cash flow that occurs at a future date.

Where zero-coupon bonds are traded the yield on a zero-coupon bond of a particular maturity is the zero-coupon rate for that maturity. Not all debt capital trading environments possess a liquid market in zero-coupon bonds. However, it is not necessary to have zero-coupon bonds in order to calculate zero-coupon rates. It is possible to calculate zero-coupon rates from a range of market rates and prices, including coupon bond yields, interest-rate futures and currency deposits.

We will illustrate shortly the close mathematical relationship between par, zero-coupon and forward rates. We will also illustrate how the boot-strapping technique could be used to calculate spot and forward rates from bond redemption yields. In addition, once the discount factors are known, any of these rates can be calculated. The relationship between the three rates allows the markets to price interest-rate swap and FRA rates, as a swap rate is the weighted arithmetic average of forward rates for the term in question.

Implied spot and forward rates[1]

In this section we describe how to obtain zero-coupon and forward interest rates from the yields available from coupon bonds, using a

---

[1] This section follows, with permission, the approach described in the book *Introduction to Option-adjusted Spread Analysis* by Tom Windas (Bloomberg Publishing 1994).

Table 7.1   Hypothetical UK government bond yields as at
7 December 2000.

Bond	Term to maturity (years)	Coupon (%)	Maturity date	Price	Gross redemption yield (%)
4% Treasury 2001	0.5	4	7-Jun-01	100	4
5% Treasury 2001	1	5	7-Dec-01	100	5
6% Treasury 2002	1.5	6	7-Jun-02	100	6
7% Treasury 2002	2	7	7-Dec-02	100	7
8% Treasury 2003	2.5	8	7-Jun-03	100	8
9% Treasury 2003	3	9%	7-Dec-03	100	9

method known as *boot-strapping*. In a government bond market such as that for US Treasuries or UK gilts, the bonds are considered to be *default-free*. The rates from a government bond yield curve describe the risk-free rates of return available in the market *today*; however, they also *imply* (risk-free) rates of return for *future time periods*. These implied future rates – known as *implied forward rates* or, simply, forward rates – can be derived from a given spot yield curve using boot-strapping. This term reflects the fact that each calculated spot rate is used to determine the next period spot rate, in successive steps.

Table 7.1 shows an hypothetical benchmark gilt yield curve for value as at 7 December 2000. The observed yields of the benchmark bonds that compose the curve are displayed in the last column. All rates are annualised and assume semi-annual compounding. The bonds all pay on the same coupon dates of 7 June and 7 December, and as the value date is a coupon date, there is no accrued interest on any of the bonds.[2] The clean and dirty prices for each bond are identical.

The gross redemption yield or *yield to maturity* of a coupon bond describes the single rate that present-values the sum of all its future cash flows to its current price. It is essentially the *internal rate of return* of the set of cash flows that make up the bond. This yield measure suffers from a fundamental weakness in that each cash flow is present-valued at the same rate, an unrealistic assumption in

---

[2] Benchmark gilts pay coupon on a semi-annual basis on 7 June and 7 December each year.

anything other than a flat yield curve environment. So, the yield to maturity is an *anticipated* measure of the return that can be expected from holding the bond from purchase until maturity. In practice, it will only be achieved under the following conditions:

- the bond is purchased on issue;
- all the coupons paid throughout the bond's life are re-invested at the same yield to maturity at which the bond was purchased;
- the bond is held until maturity.

In practice, these conditions will not be fulfilled, and so the yield to maturity of a bond is not a true interest rate for that bond's maturity period.

The bonds in Table 7.1 pay semi-annual coupons on 7 June and 7 December and have the same time period – 6 months – between 7 December 2000 (their valuation date) and 7 June 2001 (their next coupon date). However, since each issue carries a different yield, the next 6-month coupon payment for each bond is present-valued at a different rate. In other words, the 6-month bond present-values its 6-month coupon payment at its 4% yield to maturity, the 1-year at 5% and so on. Because each of these issues uses a different rate to present-value a cash flow occurring at the same future point in time, it is unclear which of the rates should be regarded as the true interest rate or benchmark rate for the 6-month period from 7 December 2000 to 7 June 2001. This problem is repeated for all other maturities.

For the purposes of valuation and analysis, however, we require a set of true interest rates, and so these must be derived from the redemption yields that we can observe from the benchmark bonds trading in the market. These rates we designate as rs_i, where rs_i is the *implied spot rate* or *zero-coupon rate* for the term beginning on 7 December 2000 and ending at the end of period i.

We begin calculating implied spot rates by noting that the 6-month bond contains only one future cash flow, the final coupon payment and the redemption payment on maturity. This means that it is in effect trading as a zero-coupon bond, as there is only one cash flow left for this bond, its final payment. Since this cash flow's present value, future value and maturity term are known, the unique interest rate that relates these quantities can be solved using the compound interest equation:

$$
\left.\begin{array}{l}
FV = PV \times \left(1 + \dfrac{rs_i}{m}\right)^{(nm)} \\[4mm]
rs_i = m \times \left(\sqrt[(nm)]{\dfrac{FV}{PV}} - 1\right)
\end{array}\right\} \tag{7.4}
$$

where FV = Future value;
PV = Present value;
rs_i = Implied i-period spot rate;
m = Number of interest periods per year;
n = Number of years in the term

The first rate to be solved is referred to as the implied 6-month spot rate and is the true interest rate for the 6-month term beginning on 2 January and ending on 2 July 2000.

Equation (7.4) relates a cash flow's present value and future value in terms of an associated interest rate, compounding convention and time period. Of course, if we re-arrange it, we may use it to solve for an implied spot rate. For the 6-month bond the final cash flow on maturity is £102, comprised of the £2 coupon payment and the £100 (*par*) redemption amount. So, we have for the first term $i = 1$, $FV = £102$, $PV = £100$, $n = 0.5$ years and $m = 2$. This allows us to calculate the spot rate as follows:

$$
\left.\begin{array}{l}
rs_i = m \times \left(\sqrt[(nm)]{FV/PV} - 1\right) \\[3mm]
rs_1 = 2 \times \left(\sqrt[(0.5\times2)]{£102/£100} - 1\right) \\[3mm]
rs_1 = 0.040\,00 \\[2mm]
rs_1 = 4.000\%
\end{array}\right\} \tag{7.5}
$$

Thus, the implied 6-month spot rate or zero-coupon rate is equal to 4%.[3] We now need to determine the implied 1-year spot rate for the term from 7 December 2000 to 7 June 2001. We note that the 1-year issue has a 5% coupon and contains two future cash flows: a £2.50 6-month coupon payment on 7 June 2001 and a £102.50 1-year coupon and principal payment on 7 December 2001. Since the first

---

[3] Of course, intuitively we could have concluded that the 6-month spot rate was 4%, without the need to apply the arithmetic, as we had already assumed that the 6-month bond was a quasi zero-coupon bond.

cash flow occurs on 7 June – 6 months from now – it must be present-valued at the 4% 6-month spot rate established above. Once this present value is determined, it may be subtracted from the £100 total present value (its current price) of the 1-year issue to obtain the present value of the 1-year coupon and cash flow. Again, we then have a single cash flow with a known present value, future value and term. The rate that equates these quantities is the implied 1-year spot rate. From Equation (7.1) the present value of the 6-month £2.50 coupon payment of the 1-year benchmark bond, discounted at the implied 6-month spot rate, is:

$$PV_{\text{6-mo cash flow,1-yr bond}} = \frac{£2.50}{\left(1 + \dfrac{0.04}{2}\right)^{(0.5 \times 2)}}$$

$$= £2.450\,98$$

The present value of the 1-year £102.50 coupon and principal payment is found by subtracting the present value of the 6-month cash flow, determined above, from the total present value (current price) of the issue:

$$PV_{\text{1-yr cash flow, 1-yr bond}} = £100 - £2.450\,98$$

$$= £97.549\,02$$

The implied 1-year spot rate is then determined by using the £97.549 02 present value of the 1-year cash flow determined above:

$$rs_2 = 2 \times \left(\sqrt[(1 \times 2)]{\frac{£102.50}{£97.549\,02}} - 1 \right)$$

$$= 0.050\,1256$$

$$= 5.012\,56\%$$

The implied 1.5-year spot rate is solved in the same way:

$$PV_{\text{6-mo cash flow, 1.5-yr bond}} = \frac{£3.00}{\left(1 + \dfrac{0.04}{2}\right)^{(0.5 \times 2)}}$$

$$= £2.941\,18$$

$$PV_{\text{1-yr cash flow, 1.5-yr bond}} = \frac{£3.00}{\left(1 + \dfrac{0.050\,1256}{2}\right)^{(1 \times 2)}}$$

$$= £2.855\,09$$

$$PV_{\text{1.5-yr cash flow, 1.5-yr bond}} = £100 - £2.941\,18 - £2.855\,09$$

$$= £94.20373$$

$$rs_3 = 2 \times \left(\sqrt[(1.5\times2)]{\frac{£103}{£94.203\,73}} - 1 \right)$$

$$= 0.060\,4071$$

$$= 6.040\,71\%$$

Extending the same process for the 2-year bond, we calculate the implied 2-year spot rate rs_4 to be 7.0906%. The implied 2.5-year and 3-year spot rates rs_5 and rs_6 are 8.1709% and 9.2879%, respectively.

The interest rates rs_1, rs_2, rs_3, rs_4, rs_5 and rs_6 describe the true zero-coupon interest rates for the 6-month, 1-year, 1.5-year, 2-year, 2.5-year and 3-year terms that begin on 7 December 2000 and end on 7 June 2001, 7 December 2001, 7 June 2002, 7 December 2002, 7 June 2003 and 7 December 2003, respectively. They are also called *implied spot rates* because they have been calculated from redemption yields observed in the market from the benchmark government bonds that were listed in Table 7.1.

Note that the 1-year, 1.5-year, 2-year, 2.5-year and 3-year implied spot rates are progressively greater than the corresponding redemption yields for these terms. This is an important result, and occurs whenever the yield curve is positively sloped. The reason for this is that the present values of a bond's shorter dated cash flows are discounted at rates that are lower than the bond's redemption yield; this generates higher present values that, when subtracted from the current price of the bond, produce a lower present value for the final cash flow. This lower present value implies a spot rate that is greater than the issue's yield. In an inverted yield curve environment we observe the opposite result – that is, implied rates that lie below the corresponding redemption yields. If the redemption yield curve is flat, the implied spot rates will be equal to the corresponding redemption yields.

Once we have calculated the spot or zero-coupon rates for the 6-month, 1-year, 1.5-year, 2-year, 2.5-year and 3-year terms, we can determine the rate of return that is implied by the yield curve for the sequence of 6-month periods beginning on 7 December 2000, 7 June 2001, 7 December 2001, 7 June 2002 and 7 December 2002. These period rates are referred to as *implied forward rates* or *forward–forward rates* and we denote these as rf_i, where rf_i is the implied 6-month forward interest rate today for the ith period.

Since the implied 6-month zero-coupon rate (spot rate) describes the return for a term that coincides precisely with the first of the series of 6-month periods, this rate describes the risk-free rate of return for the first 6-month period. It is therefore equal to the first period spot rate. Thus, we have $rf_1 = rs_1 = 4.0\%$, where rf_1 is the risk-free forward rate for the first 6-month period beginning at period 1. We show now how the risk-free rates for the second, third, fourth, fifth and sixth 6-month periods, designated rf_2, rf_3, rf_4, rf_5 and rf_6, respectively, may be solved from the implied spot rates.

The benchmark rate for the second semi-annual period rf_2 is referred to as the one-period forward 6-month rate, because it goes into effect one 6-month period from now ('one-period forward') and remains in effect for 6 months ('6-month rate'). It is therefore the 6-month rate in 6 months' time, and is also referred to as the 6-month forward–forward rate. This rate, in conjunction with the rate from the first period rf_1, must provide returns that match those generated by the implied 1-year spot rate for the entire 1-year term. In other words, £1 invested for 6 months from 7 December 2000 to 7 June 2001 at the first period's benchmark rate of 4% and then re-invested for another 6 months from 7 June 2001 to 7 December 2001 at the second period's (as yet unknown) implied *forward* rate must enjoy the same returns as £1 invested for 1 year from 7 December 2000 to 7 December 2001 at the implied 1-year *spot* rate of 5.0125%. This reflects the law of no-arbitrage.

A moment's thought will convince us that this must be so. If this were not the case, we might observe an interest-rate environment in which the return received by an investor over any given term would depend on whether an investment is made at the start period for the entire maturity term or over a succession of periods within the whole term and re-invested. If there were any discrepancies between the returns received from each approach, there would exist an unrealistic arbitrage opportunity, in which investments for a given term carrying a lower return might be sold short against the simultaneous purchase of investments for the same period carrying a higher return, thereby locking in a risk-free, cost-free profit. Therefore, forward interest rates must be calculated so that they are *arbitrage-free*. Forward rates are not therefore a prediction of what spot interest rates are likely to be in the future, rather a mathematically derived set of interest rates that reflect the current spot term structure and the rules of no-arbitrage. Excellent mathematical explanations of the no-arbitrage property of interest-rate markets are contained in Ingersoll (1987), Jarrow (1996) and Shiller (1990) among others.

The existence of a no-arbitrage market of course makes it straightforward to calculate forward rates; we know that the return from an investment made over a period must equal the return made from investing in a shorter period and successively re-investing to a matching term. If we know the return over the shorter period, we are left with only one unknown, the full-period forward rate, which is then easily calculated. In our example, having established the rate for the first 6-month period, the rate for the second 6-month period – the one-period forward 6-month rate – can be determined as below.

The future value of £1 invested at rf_1, the one-period forward rate, at the end of the first 6-month period is calculated as follows:

$$FV_1 = £1 \times \left(1 + \frac{rf_1}{2}\right)^{(0.5 \times 2)}$$

$$= £1 \times \left(1 + \frac{0.04}{2}\right)^1$$

$$= £1.020\,00$$

The future value of £1 at the end of the 1-year term, invested at the implied benchmark 1-year spot rate, is determined as follows:

$$FV_2 = £1 \times \left(1 + \frac{rs_2}{2}\right)^{(1 \times 2)}$$

$$= £1 \times \left(1 + \frac{0.050\,1256}{2}\right)^2$$

$$= £1.050\,754$$

The implied benchmark one-period forward rate rf_2 is the rate that equates the value of FV_1 (£1.02) on 7 June 2001 to FV_2 (£1.050 754) on 7 December 2001. From Equation (7.1) we have:

$$rf_2 = 2 \times \left(\sqrt[(0.5 \times 2)]{\frac{FV_2}{FV_1}} - 1\right)$$

$$= 2 \times \left(\frac{£1.050\,754}{£1.02} - 1\right)$$

$$= 0.060\,302$$

$$= 6.0302\%$$

In other words, £1 invested from 7 December to 7 June at 4.0% (the implied forward rate for the first period) and then re-invested from 7 June to 7 December 2001 at 6.0302% (the implied forward rate for the second period) would accumulate the same returns as £1 invested from 7 December 2000 to 7 December 2001 at 5.012 56% (the implied 1-year spot rate).

The rate for the third 6-month period – the two-period forward 6-month interest rate – may be calculated in the same way:

$$FV_2 = £1.050\,754$$

$$FV_3 = £1 \times \left(1 + \frac{rs_3}{2}\right)^{(1.5 \times 2)}$$

$$= £1 \times \left(1 + \frac{0.060\,4071}{2}\right)^3$$

$$= £1.093\,375$$

$$rf_3 = 2 \times \left(\sqrt[(0.5 \times 2)]{\frac{FV_3}{FV_4}} - 1 \right)$$

$$= 2 \times \left(\sqrt[1]{\frac{£1.093\,375}{£1.050\,754}} - 1 \right)$$

$$= 0.081\,125$$

$$= 8.1125\%$$

In the same way the three-period forward 6-month rate rf_4 is calculated to be 10.272 47%. The rest of the results are shown in Table 7.2. We say *one-period* forward rate because it is the forward rate that

Table 7.2   Implied spot and forward rates.

Term to maturity	Yield to maturity (%)	Implied spot rate (%)	Implied one-period forward rate (%)
0.5	4.0000	4.000 00	4.000 00
1	5.0000	5.012 56	6.030 23
1.5	6.0000	6.040 71	8.112 51
2	7.0000	7.090 62	10.272 47
2.5	8.0000	8.170 90	12.248 33
3	9.0000	9.287 92	14.556 54

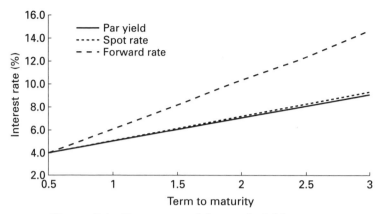

Figure 7.1   Par, spot and forward yield curves.

applies to the 6-month period. The results of the implied spot (zero-coupon) and forward rate calculations along with the given redemption yield curve are illustrated graphically in Figure 7.1.

The simple boot-strapping methodology can be applied using a spreadsheet for actual market redemption yields. However, in practice we will not have a set of bonds with exact and/or equal periods to maturity and coupons falling on the same date. Nor will they all be priced conveniently at par. In designing a spreadsheet spot rate calculator, therefore, the coupon rate and maturity date are entered as standing data and usually interpolation is used when calculating the spot rates for bonds with uneven maturity dates. Market practitioners usually use discount factors to extract spot and forward rates from market prices. For an account of this method see Choudhry *et al.* (2001, ch. 9).

THE RELATIONSHIP BETWEEN PAR, ZERO AND FORWARD RATES

There is a close mathematical relationship between par, zero-coupon and forward rates. We stated that, once the discount factors are known, any of these rates can be calculated. It is this relationship that allows the markets to price interest-rate swap and forward rate agreement (*FRA*) rates, as a swap rate is the weighted arithmetic average of forward rates for the term in question. The relationship between the zero-coupon rate and the forward rate is stated below:

One plus the zero-coupon rate is the geometric average of one plus the forward rates.

Swap rates and zero-coupon rates are both averages of the forward rates, and therefore will be very similar.

EXERCISES AND CALCULATIONS

Forward rates: break-even principle

Consider the following spot yields:

1-year	10%
2-year	12%

Assume that a bank's client wishes to lock in *today* the cost of borrowing 1-year funds in 1 year's time. The solution for the bank (and the mechanism to enable the bank to quote a price to the client) involves raising 1-year funds at 10% and investing the proceeds for 2 years at 12%. The break-even principle means that the same return must be generated from both fixed-rate and re-investment strategies.

The break-even calculation uses the following formula:

$$\left. \begin{array}{l} (1 + y_2)^2 = (1 + y_1)(1 + R) \\[2mm] R = \dfrac{(1 + y_2)^2}{(1 + y_1)} - 1 \end{array} \right\} \qquad (7.6)$$

In this example, as total funding cost must equal total return on investments (the *break-even* referred to), the quoted rate minimum is as follows:

$$(1 + 0.12)^2 = (1 + 0.10) \times (1 + R)$$

$$(1 + R) = \frac{(1 + 0.12)^2}{(1 + 0.10)}$$

$$(1 + R) = 1.140\,36$$

$$r = 14.04\%$$

This rate is the 1-year forward–forward rate, or the implied forward rate.

EXAMPLES

Example 7.1

If a 1-year AAA Eurobond trading at par yields 10% and a 2-year Eurobond of similar credit quality, also trading at par, yields 8.75%, what should be the price of a 2-year AAA zero-coupon bond? Note that Eurobonds pay coupon annually.

(a) Cost of 2-year bond (% nominal)   100

(b) *less*   Amount receivable from sale
               of first coupon on this bond
               (i.e., its present value) $= \dfrac{8.75}{1+0.10}$

                                                $= 7.95$

(c) *equals*   Amount that must be
               received on sale of second
               coupon plus principal in
               order to break even   92.05

(d) calculate the yield implied in the
    cash flows below (i.e., the 2-year
    zero-coupon yield)

    – receive   92.05
    – pay out on maturity   108.75

    Therefore $92.05 = \dfrac{108.75}{(1+R)^2}$

    Gives R equal to   8.69%

(e) What is the price of a 2-year
    zero-coupon bond with nominal
    value 100, to yield 8.69%? $= \dfrac{92.05}{108.75} \times 100$

                                             $= 84.64$

Example 7.2 The forward rate.

A highly-rated customer asks you to fix a yield at which he could issue a 2-year zero-coupon USD Eurobond in 3 years' time. At this time the US Treasury zero-coupon rates were:

1-year	6.25%
2-year	6.75%
3-year	7.00%
4-year	7.125%
5-year	7.25%

(a) Ignoring borrowing spreads over these benchmark yields, as a market maker you could cover the exposure created by borrowing funds for 5 years on a zero-coupon basis and placing these funds in the market for 3 years before lending them on to your client. Assume annual interest compounding (even if none is actually paid out during the life of the loans):

$$\text{Borrowing rate for 5 years} \left[\frac{R_5}{100}\right] = 0.0725$$

$$\text{Lending rate for 3 years} \left[\frac{R_3}{100}\right] = 0.0700$$

(b) The key arbitrage relationship is:

Total cost of funding = Total return on investments

$$(1 + R_5)^5 = (1 + R_3)^3 \times (1 + R_{3\times5})^2$$

Therefore, the break-even forward yield is:

$$R_{3\times5} = \sqrt[2]{\left[\frac{(1 + R_5)^5}{(1 + R_3)^3}\right]} - 1$$

$$= 7.63\%$$

Example 7.3   Forward rate calculation for money market term.

Consider two positions:

- repo of £100 million gilts GC from 5 November 1998 for 30 days at 5.875%;
- reverse repo of £100 million gilts GC from 5 November for 60 days at 6.125%.

The two positions can be said to be a 30-day forward 30-day (repo) interest-rate exposure (a 30- versus 60-day forward rate). What forward rate must be used if the trader wished to hedge this exposure?

The 30-day by 60-day forward rate can be calculated using the following formula:

$$R_f = \left[\left(\frac{1 + \left(Lr\% \times \dfrac{LN}{B} \right)}{1 + \left(Sr\% \times \dfrac{SN}{B} \right)} \right) - 1 \right] \times \frac{B}{Ln - Sn}$$

where R_f = Forward rate;
   $Lr\%$ = Long period rate;
   $Sr\%$ = Short period rate;
   Ln = Long period days;
   Sn = Short period days;
   B = Day-count base.

Using this formula we obtain a 30- versus 60-day forward rate of 6.3443%.

This interest-rate exposure can be hedged using interest-rate futures or FRAs. Either method is an effective hedging mechanism, although the trader must be aware of:

- the *basis* risk that exists between repo rates and the forward rates implied by futures and FRAs;
- date mismatches between expiry of futures contracts and the maturity dates of the repo transactions.

Forward rates and compounding

Examples 7.1 and 7.2 are for forward-rate calculations more than 1 year into the future, and therefore the formula used must take compounding of interest into consideration. Example 7.3 is for a forward rate within the next 12 months, with one-period bullet interest payments. A different formula is required to allow for this and is shown in the example.

FORWARD PRICING AND REPO

The principal of forward rates is used in trading to create synthetic positions. Forward pricing of short-term instruments such as T-Bills is heavily influenced by repo rates. Anomalies in pricing will occur and may present arbitrage opportunities in less liquid markets. In developed markets, forward trading is very active and greater transparency means that arbitrage opportunities are more rare.

Example 7.1 illustrated the creation of a synthetic 1-year forward–forward position. This was created by the bank going long on a 2-year position and short in the 1-year. The opposite trade would create a synthetic short position. Interest-rate futures are a transparent example of forward-rate pricing; trading interest-rate futures enables a bank to trade forward rates directly rather than synthetically via long and short deposit or bond positions. An example of an interest-rate future is the 90-day sterling interest-rate future traded on LIFFE. Being exchange-traded this is a standardised contract and its price reflects the implied 90-day interest rate as expected on the expiry day of the contract. Therefore, (100 – Price) at any time is the implied forward 3-month London Interbank Offered Rate (LIBOR) rate. FRA prices are derived directly from exchange-traded interest-rate futures.

We have seen already how forward rates are related to spot (zero-coupon) rates and yield curve modelling. Forward rates are used to price forward swaps and FRAs. The related interest-rate options (caps and floors, swaptions) also utilise the concept of the forward rate.

SELECTED REFERENCES

Choudhry, M., Joannas, D., Pereira, R. and Pienaar, R. (2001). *Capital Markets Instruments: Analysis and Valuation*. FT/Prentice Hall.

Ingersoll, J. (1987). *Theory of Financial Decision Making*. Bowman & Littlefield, ch. 18.

Jarrow, R. (1996). *Modelling Fixed Income Securities and Interest Rate Options*. McGraw-Hill, chs 2–3.

Shiller, R. (1990). The term structure of interest rates. In: Friedman, A. and Hahn, R. (eds), *Handbook of Monetary Economics*. North-Holland, ch. 13.

Windas, T. (1994). *Introduction to Option-adjusted Spread Analysis*. Bloomberg Publishing.

Chapter

8

....

THE GLOBAL MASTER REPURCHASE AGREEMENT[1]

---

[1] This chapter was co-written with Daniel Franks of Allen & Overy LLP in London. The authors are writing in their individual private capacity.

In this chapter we introduce the standard repo legal agreement under which most repo trades are carried out, the Global Master Repurchase Agreement (*GMRA*).

TBMA/ICMA AGREEMENT

The Bond Markets Association (*TBMA*) – previously called the Public Securities Association (*PSA*) – is a US-based body that originally developed the market standard documentation for repo in the US domestic market, introduced in February 1986. It developed in conjunction with the International Securities Market Association (*ISMA*) – renamed the International Capital Markets Association (*ICMA*) in October 2005 – the Global Master Repurchase Agreement. This is the market standard repo document used as the legal basis for repo in non-US dollar markets, introduced in November 1992. It was updated 3 years later to include UK gilts, buy/sell transactions and relevant agency annexes.

The agreement covers transactions between parties including repo, buy/sell-back and agency trades, and has adapted for securities paying net, as well as for equities.

The key features of the agreement are that:

- repo trades are structured as outright sales and repurchases;
- full ownership is conferred on securities transferred;
- there is an obligation to return 'equivalent' securities;
- there is provision for initial and variation margin;
- coupon is paid over to the repo seller at the time of payment;
- legal title to collateral is confirmed in the event of default.

The main advantages of the agreement are:

1. Its allowance for close-out and netting are capital-efficient for Capital Adequacy Directive (*CAD*) purposes.
2. Specifying action in the event of default.
3. Its rules on margining.

THE GLOBAL MASTER REPURCHASE AGREEMENT[2]

Scope

The GMRA, jointly published by TBMA[3] and ICMA[4], is the market standard agreement for documenting sale and repurchase transactions (repos) and buy/sell-backs in the domestic and cross-border arena. While there were previous forms of the GMRA (the first version was published in November 1992 and the most recent before the 2000 version was published in 1995), the 2000 version has superseded those earlier versions. The 1995 version is still used, but significant improvements in the 2000 version have resulted in the latter being the preferred choice for the majority of new trading relationships.

While the GMRA is governed by English law, its scope is not limited to the English repo market. Rather, it is widely used in the European and other domestic and cross-border repo markets. TBMA also published the 1996 Master Repurchase Agreement (MRA) governed by New York law. While the MRA is substantially similar to the GMRA in terms of structure and language, it is predominantly used in the US domestic and, to a lesser extent, cross-border market. The MRA was initially designed for documenting repos of US Treasury and agency securities, but the most recent version encompasses a broad range of securities.

In addition, certain European countries with developed repo markets have their own methods of trading and have produced their own forms of documentation. For example, the French and German markets have produced their own forms of agreement. However, since the GMRA is not designed specifically for one jurisdiction or one type of security, it is the market standard in terms of cross-border repo documentation.

This section focuses on the GMRA governed by English law, although many of the issues discussed in this chapter will apply

---

[2] This section was written by Daniel Franks of Allen & Overy LLP, London. The views, thoughts and opinions herein represent those of the authors in their individual private capacity.
[3] Formerly the Public Securities Association (PSA).
[4] Formerly the International Securities Markets Association (ISMA).

equally to its New York law equivalent and to the other types of repo documentation in the market.

STRUCTURE

The GMRA is structured as a master netting agreement under which the parties can enter into one or more repos. It consists of a pre-printed standard form master agreement containing provisions that are applicable to all repos between the parties, a number of annexes and a confirmation for each transaction.

The legal and credit relationship of the parties is contained in the pre-printed form and in the annexes (although note the product-specific annexes referred to below). As either party may be buyer or seller in relation to any given repo, the GMRA is generic in that it applies equally to each party and does not seek to favour either party. If the parties wish to amend the standard provisions of the GMRA, they are able to do so in Annex I, where they are also required to make certain elections for the purposes of the pre-printed standard form. Parties frequently seek to amend or adapt the GMRA to reflect their internal policies or practices or to reflect their relative credit strengths. Towards the end of this chapter there is a discussion of some of the key areas of the GMRA that market participants frequently seek to amend.

The economic terms of a repo will be set out in the confirmation relating to that transaction, including who is buyer and who is seller in relation to that transaction. Parties should refrain from including in individual confirmations any provision which is intended to reflect their general trading relationship, as such a provision should be included in Annex I (or, if subsequent to execution of the GMRA, in an amendment agreement). This would more accurately reflect the structure of the documentation, which anticipates relationship matters being included in the master agreement and transaction-specific matters being included in the relevant confirmation.

The parties may also incorporate other annexes which, like the GMRA itself, are pre-printed and standard form. These annexes have been published by various bodies either for use with particular types of counterparty or where the parties intend to repo particular types of security.

Examples of counterparty-specific annexes are: the *Netherlands Annex*, which is published jointly by TBMA and ICMA for use where both parties are incorporated in the Netherlands; and the *South African Annex*, which is published by ICMA for use where one of the parties is incorporated in the Republic of South Africa.

Examples of product-specific annexes are: the *Gilts Annex*, published by the Bank of England for use where the parties intend to repo gilt-edged securities; and the *Equities Annex* and *Italian Annex*, each of which is published jointly by TBMA and ICMA, for use where the parties intend to repo equities or securities issued in Italy, respectively. Other standard form annexes are available for use, and a full list of annexes is available at *www.icma.org*

KEY PRINCIPLES

As is the case with any master agreement, certain key principles underpin the way in which the GMRA operates. While there are many important aspects to the GMRA, each of which has its own consequences, these key principles are fundamental to the relationship between the parties and the way in which the GMRA and transactions entered into under it would be treated by the courts.

These key principles are title transfer, netting (including the 'single agreement' concept and early termination and close-out netting) and margin maintenance. Each of these is discussed briefly below.

Title transfer

A repo is, in legal terms, the sale of securities from the seller to the buyer and the repurchase of those or fungible securities[5] by the seller from the buyer at a future time. Each of the sale and repurchase elements of the transaction are effected by way of 'true sale'; that is, full title is transferred from one party to the other. While the seller retains economic exposure to the securities, he divests himself of any proprietary interest in the securities themselves; once the seller has sold the securities to the buyer, the seller simply has a debt claim against the buyer for the delivery of fungible equivalent securities.

---

[5] That is, securities of the same issuer, part of the same issue and of an identical type, nominal value, description and amount as the securities originally purchased.

In economic terms, however, repos resemble secured financing arrangements. The buyer provides financing to the seller on the purchase date in return for the delivery of securities. On the repurchase date, the seller pays the repurchase price in return for the delivery by the buyer of securities. A secured loan has similar characteristics in terms of the flow of cash and assets: on the drawdown date, the lender provides financing to the borrower in return for collateral; on the repayment date of the loan, the lender releases the collateral upon repayment by the borrower of the drawn funds. To complete the analogy, the seller in a repo is borrowing funds and providing collateral (the securities); the buyer is lending funds and receiving collateral.

The key legal distinction between a repo and a secured loan lies in the concept of title transfer: a secured loan typically involves the borrower retaining a form of proprietary interest in the securities provided as collateral; in a repo, after selling the securities, the seller has no proprietary interest in the securities and simply has a debt claim against the buyer.

Recharacterisation

The characterisation of a transaction either as a true sale and repurchase (i.e., a repo) or as a secured financing is important, as the characterisation may, depending on the relevant laws,[6] result in different outcomes in terms of validity, enforceability and priority of the parties' interests and those of third parties. For example, whether the buyer obtains outright title to the securities, or whether he simply has a security interest in them, will affect the rights of any third party who seeks to acquire those securities from him.

In addition, it is necessary in many jurisdictions to 'perfect' a security interest, which is to take steps in order for the security interest to be enforceable against, and have priority in relation to, a liquidator or creditors of the person who granted the security. If a court were to

---

[6] The conflict-of-laws rules, otherwise known as private international law, of any country will determine which jurisdiction is relevant for the purposes of the relationship between the parties and their respective interests in the securities. These rules, which typically distinguish between proprietary rights and contractual or other personal rights, are often complex and are beyond the scope of this chapter.

recharacterise a transaction as a secured financing arrangement, then failure to take these steps may make the transfer of the securities invalid. Where the transaction does not involve a security interest, such as a true sale and repurchase transaction, then these perfection requirements may not be relevant.

There may also be enforcement restrictions that are applicable to the security interest – for example, a freeze – requirements for a judicial sale by public auction or a compulsory grace period. Each of these may not be applicable to repos to the extent that they are characterised as true sale and repurchase transactions.

In addition to the legal disadvantages, there may be a number of practical disadvantages that would ensue if a repo were to be recharacterised as a secured financing arrangement rather than as a true sale and repurchase. For example, the seller may be subject to a negative pledge or borrowing limits in his credit facility agreements which prevent him from borrowing funds or from granting security. Provided these restrictions or limits are not drafted so as to capture true sale and repurchase transactions, then a repo may not contravene these provisions.

As such, it is likely to be important to the parties that repos are characterised as a true sale and repurchase and are not recharacterised as secured financing arrangements. The English courts accord considerable respect to the characterisation given by the parties themselves and will only recharacterise where the express characterisation is either a sham or at odds with the legal substance of the relations created in the GMRA. As such, the GMRA contains language that expressly demonstrates the parties' intention that each repo is a true sale and repurchase transaction. The GMRA provides that all title to and interest in the securities is transferred by the seller to the buyer. Once the buyer has purchased the securities, the seller no longer has any proprietary or legal interest in them (although he will, of course, retain economic exposure to their value by virtue of the repurchase element of the repo) and the buyer is free to deal with the securities in his ordinary course of business. Upon the repurchase date, the buyer is obliged simply to deliver fungible securities, rather than being obliged to deliver the exact same securities as he received.

Whether a repo is likely to be recharacterised as a secured financing depends on all laws that may be relevant, including the local insolvency laws of the counterparty. In relation to the European markets, the Financial Collateral Directive[7] requires member states of the European Union to introduce legislation which, among other things, removes perfection requirements in relation to certain types of financial transaction with certain types of institution and which provides for title transfer arrangements to take effect in accordance with their terms, thereby removing the scope for recharacterisation. While the local legislation enacted by the relevant member state will determine whether repos constitute one of the relevant financial contracts, the Financial Collateral Directive expressly includes repurchase agreements within its scope and a member state would have failed properly to implement the Financial Collateral Directive if local legislation were not to take the same approach.

In order to assist their members in determining the characterisation of repos, TBMA and ICMA have commissioned legal opinions from counsel in a number of jurisdictions. Counsel were requested to opine on, among other things, whether the GMRA would be recognised as a true sale and repurchase or whether there is a risk that the courts in the relevant jurisdiction would recharacterise the agreement as a secured financing arrangement. At the time of going to press, TBMA and ICMA have obtained opinions from counsel in 21 jurisdictions. A full list of opinions and the text of those opinions are available to TBMA/ICMA members at TBMA and ICMA's websites. In order for TBMA or ICMA's members to obtain the benefit of the opinions, it is important to ensure that the counterparty is of a type covered by the opinion and that the terms of the GMRA necessary for the giving of the opinion have not been amended.

To the extent that parties seek to amend certain key provisions of the GMRA, they should bear in mind the impact, if any, of the amendments on the risk that the transactions are recharacterised as secured financing arrangements. In particular, parties should be cautious when faced with provisions which remove the buyer's right to deal freely in the securities during the term of the transaction, which require the buyer to deliver identical (as opposed to fungible equivalent) securities or which allow the seller to substitute the securities without the consent of the buyer, particularly in relation to a hold-in-custody repo. Each of these factors, of itself, may not necessarily result in recharacterisation, as the question will (at least under English law) be whether the parties intended a true sale to be

---

[7] Directive 2002/47/EC of the European Parliament and of the Council of 6 June 2002 on financial collateral arrangements.

effected. However, the courts are likely to look at these and other surrounding factors to determine whether the intention was to create a secured financing arrangement and whether the actual relationship is at odds with the characterisation given by the parties in the GMRA.

Master netting agreement

The GMRA is a master netting agreement; that is, an agreement that replaces gross payment or delivery obligations in respect of one or more transactions between the parties with a net payment or delivery obligation. The GMRA contains two types of netting arrangement: settlement netting and close-out netting.

Settlement netting

The settlement netting provision of the GMRA provides that, if on any day amounts in the same currency are due between the parties in respect of one or more repos (or in respect of a margin call, discussed below), the obligations of the parties to make those gross payments are replaced with an obligation to make a single net payment. Similarly, if on any day fungible securities are required to be transferred between the parties in respect of one or more repos (or in respect of a margin call), the obligations of the parties to make those transfers are combined in a single calculation of a net quantity of securities to be transferred.

The object of settlement netting is to reduce settlement risk; that is, the risk that one party pays a currency or transfers securities and the other party becomes insolvent before paying the currency or transferring the securities that he is required to pay or transfer. It can also reduce the administrative burden of making gross payments or deliveries and the associated transaction costs.

Close-out netting and the 'single agreement'

Close-out netting under the GMRA operates by providing that, upon a default by one party of an obligation under the GMRA, all obligations of the parties under the GMRA are accelerated and valued so that they are converted into sums owing between the parties. Upon a close-out, the sums owing by one party are set off against the sums owing by the other party so that only the resulting net balance is payable. Thus, early termination and set-off are used to achieve close-out netting.

As discussed above, the seller of securities under a repo does not, after the purchase date, retain any proprietary interest in the securities. Accordingly, his exposure is not simply an economic exposure to the value of the securities but also a credit exposure to the buyer; if the buyer fails to deliver securities on the repurchase date, the seller simply has a debt claim against the buyer. Similarly, the buyer may have a credit exposure to the seller if the value of the securities falls during the terms of the repo.

The GMRA seeks to reduce credit exposure in two ways: the first, discussed below under 'Margin maintenance', is to provide for mark-to-market margining; the second is close-out netting, which is of particular importance when seeking to reduce credit exposure upon the insolvency of a counterparty.

Close-out netting seeks to reduce credit exposure both within and without the insolvency context. Pre-insolvency, the GMRA seeks to ensure that one party is not required to perform gross payment or delivery obligations while waiting for the other party to perform his own gross obligations (the first party thereby taking the credit risk of non-performance by the other).

However, while the protection afforded by close-out netting pre-insolvency is, of course, important, it is perhaps even more so upon the onset of insolvency proceedings of one of the parties. Close-out netting seeks to reduce credit exposure by reducing the risk of a liquidator (or similar official) of an insolvent party 'cherry-picking'. 'Cherry-picking' is, in essence, where the liquidator of an insolvent party insists that the solvent party performs his obligations in full in respect of those transactions which are profitable to the insolvent party and requires the solvent party to claim as an unsecured creditor for those transactions which are onerous to the insolvent party. The solvent party's exposure, when cherry-picked, is gross. Close-out netting is designed to ensure that, instead of maintaining a gross exposure, the solvent party has only a net exposure against the insolvent party.

In addition to the aim of reducing credit risk on a counterparty, close-out netting may result in reduced capital adequacy costs. If the regulator of a party is satisfied that, upon the insolvency of his counterparty, the party will maintain a net, rather than gross, credit exposure, then the regulatory capital required to be set aside in relation to the trading relationship may be lower. Reduced credit exposure will also be important for banks with limited credit lines.

The provisions of the GMRA designed to reduce the risk of cherry-picking are not limited to early termination and close-out. The GMRA also contains a statement of the intention of the parties to establish interdependence between all transactions entered into under the GMRA. The pre-printed form of the GMRA, together with all annexes and all transactions and their confirmations, constitutes one single agreement. The purpose of the 'single agreement' is to ensure that, if a liquidator has the ability to disclaim an onerous contract, its ability to do so is limited to the net sum due after close-out netting because none of the gross claims under individual transactions are themselves contracts; rather, they form part of a larger, single contract.

The enforceability of close-out netting against an insolvent person will therefore depend on whether the insolvency laws applicable to that person recognise the validity of the single agreement principle and of early termination and close-out netting. If the applicable insolvency laws were not to recognise their validity, the result would be that it would not be possible to net all outstanding positions, allowing the liquidator to cherry-pick.

Some jurisdictions do not allow a solvent party to cancel or terminate contracts with an insolvent party, particularly if the insolvent party is subject to a rehabilitation procedure where contracts are considered necessary for the success of the rehabilitation. Many jurisdictions prohibit set-off upon insolvency as they consider set-off to be a way of preferring the solvent party above all other unsecured creditors. Other jurisdictions (e.g., England and Wales) allow both early termination and set-off.

Many jurisdictions have created special netting statutes limited to financial markets, which allow early termination and close-out netting for specific financial contracts in favour of specific institutions. For example, France, Germany, Italy and the United States each have enacted legislation permitting close-out netting in relation to certain types of transaction and institution. In addition, in relation to the European markets, the Financial Collateral Directive referred to above requires member states of the European Union to introduce legislation permitting the enforceability of early termination and close-out netting of specific types of financial contract (including repos, as discussed above) upon the insolvency of particular types of institution.

As such, when entering into a GMRA with a counterparty, it is important to consider whether the early termination and close-out netting provisions of the GMRA would be valid and enforceable upon the insolvency of the counterparty. Indeed, if a party wishes to benefit from reduced capital adequacy requirements, its regulator is likely to require the party first to satisfy a number of conditions, including obtaining a reasoned legal opinion. In the opinions commissioned by TBMA and ICMA, discussed above, counsel were requested to opine on the validity and enforceability of the GMRA, including its early termination and close-out netting provisions. Again, in order for TBMA or ICMA's members to obtain the benefit of the opinions, it is important to ensure that the counterparty is of a type covered by the opinion and that the terms of the GMRA necessary for the giving of the opinion have not been amended.

Margin maintenance

As the value of securities may fluctuate and the repo rate accrues daily, there may on any day be a difference between the value of each party's future contingent obligations (i.e., the obligation of the seller to pay the repurchase price and the buyer to deliver securities). In addition, the parties may apply a 'haircut' to the value of the securities in order to discount their value to reflect volatility. By comparing the market value (after application of the haircut) of the purchased securities to the amount of cash payable at the date when one is marking-to-market, it can be determined which party has an exposure to the other in relation to any particular transaction and would suffer a loss were the other party to default. The party which is in the position of suffering a potential loss (once the aggregate of his transaction exposures and other amounts owing to him are taken into account) has a counterparty exposure and may call for margin[8] to collateralise his exposure.

As the credit risk on a counterparty to a repo is intended to be relatively low, to reflect the fact that the repo economically resembles a secured financing arrangement, the GMRA contains provisions allowing the parties to mark their positions to market on a daily, or even more frequent, basis and request margin to be provided.

---

[8] Or 'collateral' – the terms are used interchangeably in the market and in this chapter, although the GMRA is drafted with reference to 'margin'.

The GMRA provides for an outright transfer of collateral so that, as with the purchased securities which are the subject of the repo, the recipient of the collateral asset is free to deal with it and is required to return only a fungible equivalent.

The GMRA treats margin as an independent obligation of the parties, distinct from their obligations in respect of any individual transaction. The parties calculate their net exposure across all outstanding transactions and make a payment or delivery of margin to collateralise any exposure.

As an alternative to the net margin maintenance provisions, the GMRA contains other options should the parties not wish to provide margin on a net basis. First, the parties may decide to margin individual transactions on a gross basis (while margining other transactions on a net basis). Second, the parties may wish to re-price the transaction to reflect the then-current value of the securities (upon which, a cash payment will be due between the parties equal to the difference in value between the re-priced transaction and the 'new' transaction). Finally, the parties may wish to adjust or amend the transaction entirely, in which case the old transaction is unwound and a new transaction entered into in relation to agreed new securities.

Each of these options affords the parties differing degrees of flexibility. In particular, the adjustment of a transaction allows the parties to amend the transaction without affecting the underlying cash return. Each adjustment and re-pricing allow the parties economically to reduce exposure to the other party even though they may not have systems in place to calculate exposure on a daily basis or serve or satisfy a margin call.

NEGOTIATION OF THE GMRA

As with any type of agreement, parties to a GMRA are likely to negotiate its terms before it is executed. These negotiations are typically less lengthy than negotiations of, say, an ISDA Master Agreement, but nonetheless each party will have to consider the terms of the GMRA and whether any amendments are required to reflect his commercial intention.

Below is a brief discussion of some of the key provisions of the GMRA which are negotiated between the parties.

Margin maintenance

The parties to the GMRA are likely to require the margin maintenance provisions to be negotiated, to the greatest extent possible, in
accordance with the demands of their collateral management functions and to maintain consistency across their documentation.

In particular, the parties should consider the frequency of marking
to market, valuation sources and timing, the types of asset that are
acceptable as collateral and the requirements regarding the delivery
period of margin calls.

Frequency of marking-to-market and valuation

The GMRA does not specify a limit in terms of the frequency of
marking-to-market. The margin maintenance provisions of the
GMRA are defined by reference to one party's exposure to the other
'at any time' and, therefore, allow parties to manage intra-day movements in prices.

The GMRA provides a standard mechanism for the valuation of
securities – namely, the price for those securities at any time on
any day obtained from a generally recognised pricing source. The
parties to the GMRA may wish to increase the certainty that a
particular pricing source is acceptable, either by limiting the available pricing sources to a specified list or by providing that particular
sources shall always be considered acceptable. While a definitive list
would reduce flexibility (although the parties would be free to agree
an alternative on a case-by-case basis), providing fallbacks in Annex I
would reduce the scope for dispute.

Eligible collateral

Collateral can either be in the form of cash (known as 'cash margin')
or securities (known as 'margin securities'). Save for cash margin in
the base currency, which the parties are required to specify in Annex
I, the GMRA does not contain a list of which types of asset are
acceptable as collateral.

Securities are only eligible as collateral if they are reasonably acceptable to the party making the margin call. If the parties wish to ensure
that a specific type of security will always be acceptable as collateral,
then they should make provision for this in Annex I.

Cash collateral must be provided either in the base currency or in any other currency agreed between the parties. Again, if the parties wish to ensure that cash denominated in a specific currency (other than the base currency) will always be acceptable, then they should make provision for this in Annex I.

Each party should, however, bear in mind that, other than where the party making the margin call has previously provided collateral and has not had collateral returned (in which case he may specify in the margin call that the collateral be in the same form as was previously provided), the composition of a margin transfer is at the option of the party making the transfer. As such, a party should not specify as eligible collateral any assets or currencies which he is not prepared to receive.

Delivery period

If the parties fail to specify in Annex I a delivery period for margin calls, then the fallback under the GMRA is the minimum period as is customarily required for the settlement or delivery of the relevant cash or securities. There are both advantages and disadvantages to specifying a specific period rather than relying on customary practice: applying a specific period provides certainty and avoids potential disputes over what is customary. However, there is a risk that a definitive period specified in Annex I may fall out of step with market practice. This may be of particular concern either to the party calling for margin, if settlement periods in the market become shorter than the period specified in Annex I, or to the party required to deliver margin, if settlement periods in the market become longer than the period specified in Annex I.

If the parties wish to identify a specific period, each party should consider the latest time by which he is able to receive a margin call and the shortest period within which he is able to satisfy that margin call. Similarly, each party should consider the period within which he would expect his counterparty to be required to provide collateral following a margin call.

For example, if a party is unable to source a particular type of security or cash denominated in a particular currency at short notice, then a provision in Annex I (were the parties to include one) which allows for demands to be made at, say, 16:00 hours local time and which requires the delivery of collateral on the same day that demand is made, is unlikely to be suitable. As such, the parties typically only specify as eligible collateral those assets or currencies which are relatively quick to source and specify in Annex I a delivery period by reference to asset type and the time of receipt of the margin call.

Margin threshold

The margin maintenance provisions of the GMRA do not contain a *de minimis* threshold before collateral is required to be delivered. In practice, margin calls are often not made until a party's net exposure has exceeded a certain level. This may either be because a party is willing to take a degree of credit exposure on his counterparty, or because he considers the costs and administrative burdens associated with requesting and delivering collateral make margin calls to cover low exposures unduly burdensome. Parties may therefore wish to include in Annex I a provision that expressly provides that a party may not make a margin call unless his net exposure to the other party exceeds a threshold. This threshold is typically determined either by reference to a fixed level, or by reference to the aggregate of all purchase prices across all repos between the parties, or by reference to both. Each party should then consider whether, if net exposure were to exceed the threshold, only the balance is required to be collateralised, or whether the full exposure is required to be collateralised.

Failure to deliver

The 2000 version of the GMRA, unlike the 1995 version, contains an event of default which is breached if a party fails to deliver securities in a timely manner. This event of default is optional and will not apply unless the parties specify it as applicable in Annex I.

Some market participants favour the inclusion of this event of default as they consider that a failure to deliver securities is often an important early indication of credit deterioration or potential insolvency (although this may not be the reason that a particular failure to deliver actually occurs in a particular case). Other market participants do not favour the provision because they consider that 'settlement fails' are common and generally do not indicate a credit deterioration. In particular, a short squeeze on the securities may make it difficult to source the securities for a substantial period of time and these market participants consider that an event beyond their control and affecting the market generally should not trigger an event of default entitling the other party to close out all outstanding repos (and potentially trigger a cross-default clause).

When considering whether to specify the failure-to-deliver event of default as applicable, each party should bear in mind that the GMRA contains (in addition to the optional event of default) a 'mini close-out' provision which entitles the non-defaulting party to take certain action in relation to individual transactions affected by a failure to deliver. This action includes the ability to terminate the affected transactions. As such, each party will have a remedy in relation to individual transactions should the other party fail to deliver securities, notwithstanding that the event of default may not be specified as applicable. In addition, if the event of default is specified as applicable, the parties may also wish to consider including a grace period before the non-defaulting party can terminate all outstanding repos.

CONDITION PRECEDENT

The 2000 version of the GMRA contains an optional condition precedent which allows a party to withhold all payments or deliveries (other than payment of a close-out amount) where an event of default has occurred in respect of the other party (or would occur if the non-defaulting party were to serve notice). Again, this is a provision that was not included in the 1995 version.

This condition precedent is similar to the approach taken in the ISDA Master Agreement and is a useful 'flawed asset' provision. Among other things, its aim is to reduce the risk of cherry-picking, since the insolvent (and defaulting) party's claim against the solvent party is flawed in that it is contingent upon the event of default being cured.

As with the concept of early termination and close-out netting, the flawed asset should be used with caution in jurisdictions which prohibit insolvency set-off, due to the risk of recharacterisation as a way of preferring the solvent party above all other unsecured creditors. In addition, each party should consider whether a non-defaulting party should be required to perform in circumstances where the other party is in default but has performed in full all his outstanding obligations (thereby resulting in the non-defaulting party having no credit exposure).

Set-off

Parties may wish to consider including a set-off provision which entitles a non-defaulting party to offset an amount owing under the GMRA (after early termination and close-out netting) against any other amounts owed between the parties under other arrangements – for example, a loan facility agreement or an ISDA Master Agreement. A set-off provision is of value where the parties are solvent or where one party is insolvent but his local insolvency law does not provide for mandatory set-off.

Automatic early termination

The insolvency event of default in the GMRA provides for automatic early termination (i.e., termination without the need for notice by the non-defaulting party) in certain cases. Automatic early termination has a number of potential disadvantages for a solvent counter-party dealing with a potentially insolvent defaulting party.

The principal disadvantage is the loss of flexibility for the non-defaulting party, at a time when the non-defaulting party may wish to preserve his ability to control the timing of early termination and close-out, so as to maximise his bargaining strength in any possible work-out with the defaulting party.

The supposed advantage of automatic early termination is that it increases the likelihood that the early termination and close-out provisions of the GMRA will be triggered before the commencement of formal insolvency proceedings, although whether, in a particular case, the close-out is triggered pre-commencement will depend on the relevant facts. In many jurisdictions, close-out netting is enforceable both before and after commencement of insolvency proceedings.

As such, each party should consider whether the practical disadvantages of automatic early termination outweigh the advantages and, if appropriate, remove the automatic nature of the event of default.

PRODUCT- AND COUNTERPARTY-SPECIFIC AMENDMENTS AND ADDITIONAL ANNEXES

Finally, each party should consider whether any amendments are required in light of the type of entity with which he is dealing or the securities which are to be purchased. For example, additional provisions or specific amendments may be required for entities such as sovereigns, building societies, insurance companies or hedge funds. The GMRA is also unsuitable for use with illiquid securities or securities with no identifiable market – for example, certain credit-linked securities.

In this regard, each party should consider whether any of the standard form annexes, referred to above, are required. Each party should also consult their legal advisers in all relevant jurisdictions – for example, the jurisdiction of the governing law of the contract (England), the jurisdiction where the counterparty is incorporated or where the securities are located. The property laws, contract laws and conflict-of-laws rules in the relevant jurisdictions are likely to determine the characterisation of the agreement and its enforceability against the parties.

GILT REPO LEGAL AGREEMENT

The Gilt Repo Legal Agreement is an amended version of the revised (November 1995) BMA/ICMA agreement for the UK gilt repo market. The BMA/ICMA agreement was extended with supplemental terms and conditions for gilt repo forming Part 2 to Annex I of the BMA/ICMA agreement and modified by a side letter in connection with the upgrade to the Central Gilts Office (CGO; see §12.8 of Annex I) service in November 1997.

Participants in the gilt repo market are strongly recommended to adopt the Gilt Repo Legal Agreement for gilt repo transactions, as set out in the *Gilt Repo Code of Best Practice* (§12.9). The Code was issued by the Bank of England. Use of the legal agreement is subject to legal confirmation of its effectiveness, if the specific circumstances in which it is to be used are not straightforward. The agreement is recommended as the umbrella documentation for all types of repo, including buy/sell-back.

The agreement provides for the following:

- the absolute transfer of title to securities;
- daily marking-to-market;
- appropriate initial margin and for maintenance of margin whenever the mark to market reveals a material change of value;
- clear events of default and the consequential rights and obligations of the counterparties;
- in the event of default, full set-off of claims between counterparties;
- clarification of rights of parties regarding substitution of collateral and the treatment of coupon payments;
- terms subject to English law.

These summarise the provisions as contained in the BMA/ICMA agreement.

SELECTED REFERENCES

BoE (1995). *Gilts Annex*. Bank of England, November.

BoE (1995). *Gilt Repo Code of Best Practice* (§12.9). Bank of England, November.

ICMA (2000). *South African Annex*. International Capital Markets Association.

TBMA/ICMA (1999). *Equities Annex*. The Bond Markets Association/ International Capital Markets Association.

TBMA/ICMA (2000). *Netherlands Annex*. The Bond Markets Association/ International Capital Markets Association.

TBMA/ICMA (2000). *Italian Annex*. The Bond Markets Association/International Capital Markets Association.

Chapter

9

ACCOUNTING, TAX AND REGULATORY CAPITAL ISSUES IN REPO

In this chapter we introduce issues of a regulatory, accounting, tax and capital nature associated with repo. They are introduced in overview fashion only because their specialised nature places them outside the scope of this book.

ACCOUNTING, TAX AND CAPITAL ISSUES

Accounting

The accounting treatment of repos reflects the commercial substance of the transaction, which is as a *secured loan*. For tax purposes the transfer of securities at the start of the trade does not count as a disposal, which tallies with the accounting treatment. However, tax treatment is different for the income in a repo. As a collateralised financing transaction, repos are on-balance sheet transactions. In a repo transaction for the seller, bonds given as collateral remain on the balance sheet of the seller. The corresponding liability is the repo cash. Coupon continues to accrue to the seller. The opposite is the case for the buyer. As an accounting entry a repo appears as a secured loan and not an actual sell transaction.

With regard to the profit & loss account, the repo interest (repo return) is treated as the payment of interest and is taken as a charge on an accruals basis – that is, it is entered in the books at the time of the transaction.

Taxation

The tax treatment of repo differs in each jurisdiction. In the UK the return on the cash leg of a repo is treated as interest and is taxed as income. Coupon payments during the term of a repo are treated for tax purposes as being to the benefit of the counterparty, the taxable date of which is taken to be the dividend date. When trading in overseas markets where the tax treatment is uncertain, institutions must investigate the principal tax issues, both from the point of view of repo seller and buyer:

- *Repo seller* – for the seller, the principal issue is whether the 'sale' of securities will trigger a taxable event and/or result in transfer taxes. The type of institution engaged in the trade may affect the resulting tax treatment, as it may be taxable or tax-exempt, as will the firm's country of residence, as there may be a form of double-taxation treaty. For a cross-border trade the accounting treatment in both countries must be taken into consideration, and whether the repo is treated as a sale or not. The basic accounting treatment is that a repo is not a sale – however, this is not the case in all countries.

• *Repo buyer* – for the buyer, the principal issue to ascertain is whether the 'purchase' of securities will result in transfer taxes.

A taxation issue may arise whenever a coupon payment is made during the term of a repo. If a repo runs over a record date (coupon date) a 'manufactured dividend' will arise. In the UK this is treated as income accruing to the beneficial owner of the securities, and therefore not the income of the cash lender. For this reason the dividend is deductible for the cash lender. There is an additional issue if the coupon is actually paid net of any withholding taxes or gross. The coupon on government bonds is usually paid gross, the major exception is Japanese Government bonds which pay coupon net. The UK only recently introduced gross payment of coupon (previously foreign-domiciled investors had to register to receive gross coupons). However, holders are still liable to tax which is paid in the normal course of tax assessment.

CAPITAL TREATMENT

In this section we discuss treatment under Basel I. The next section discusses treatment under Basel II which is due for implementation during 2007 and 2008, depending on the particular jurisdiction.

Capital Adequacy Directive

The Bank for International Settlements (*BIS*) originally introduced a standard for capital adequacy in July 1988. This was known as the Basel Capital Accord or Capital Adequacy Directive (*CAD*) and specified a relatively uniform system for defining exactly how much capital a bank required. The rules came into effect at the end of 1992. They set a minimum ratio of capital to *weighted risk assets* of 8%. Each asset on the bank's balance sheet is assigned a weighting, which can be from 0% for assets considered riskless, to 100% for the most risky assets. For example, most interbank deposits are given a 20% weighting, while most bank lending receives the full 100% weighting. A £100 million corporate loan would therefore consume £8 million of the bank's capital (i.e., the bank would have to set aside £8m against the loan), while a £100 million interbank deposit would require a £1.6 million allocation of bank capital. The risk weighting applied varies with the type of counterparty; broadly speaking, the weightings are:

0%   Cash, Zone A central governments/banks
20%   EIB, Zone B credit institutions
50%   Fully secured loans
100%   Zone A or Zone B non-bank sectors (e.g., corporates).

An institution's capital charge calculation is therefore:

Principal value × Risk Weighting × Capital charge [8%]

The sum of the exposures is taken. Firms may use netting or portfolio modelling to reduce the total principal value.

The capital requirements for off-balance sheet instruments are lower because for these instruments the *principal* is rarely at risk. Interest-rate derivatives such as forward rate agreements (*FRAs*) of less than 1 year's maturity have no capital requirement at all, while a long-term currency swap requires capital of between 0.08% and 0.2% of the nominal principal. For example, a £100 million 5-year currency swap between banks would require capital allocation of £80,000. This is considerably lower than the transactions considered above.

The BIS makes a distinction between *banking book* transactions as carried out by retail and commercial banks (primarily deposits and lending) and *trading book* transactions as carried out by investment banks and securities houses. Capital treatment sometimes differs between banking and trading books.

CAD treatment for repo

A repo transaction attracts a charge on the *trading book*. The formula for calculating capital allocation is:

$$CA = \max\{[(C_{mv} - S_{mv}) \times 8\% \times RW], 0\}$$

where C_{mv} = Value of cash proceeds;
            S_{mv} = Market value of securities;
            RW = Counterparty risk weighting (as percentage).

Example 9.1   CAD example.

The CAD charge for a repo transaction with the following terms:

Clean price of collateral	100
Accrued interest	0
Cash proceeds on £50m nominal	£50,000,000
Counterparty	OECD bank
Counterparty risk weighting	20%

$$CA = \{[(50,000,000 - 50,000,000) \times 8\% \times 20\%], 0\}$$
$$= 0$$

The CAD charge for a loan/deposit transaction of the same size is as follows:

Unsecured loan	£50,000,000
Counterparty	OECD bank
Counterparty risk weighting	20%

$$CA = \max\{[50,000,000 \times 8\% \times 20\%], 0\}$$
$$= £800,000$$

Balance sheet implications

Repo conducted under legal documentation, such as the BMA/ICMA agreement, are given favourable treatment for CAD purposes compared with undocumented repo. Buy/sell-backs attract the full charge based on the counterparty risk weighting. Documented repos attract a capital charge at the counterparty risk weighting based on the mark-to-market value of all positions between the parties.

THE BASEL II FRAMEWORK

The BIS Basel II rules were published in final form in June 2004 with implementation set for 2007 or possibly 2008 in certain jurisdictions. Here we present some highlights on the framework.

Basel II framework

Compared with the Basel I regime, general market opinion holds that the Basel II rules are an improved benchmark for assessing capital adequacy relative to bank risk. The broad objectives of Basel II remain as they were at the start of the formulation process.

The basic internal risk-based (*IRB*) framework including the three-pillar structure described at its first draft has remained in place in the final draft. A significant change was the decision to base the capital charges for all asset classes on unexpected loss (*UL*) only, and not on both UL and expected loss (*EL*). In other words, banks must hold sufficient reserves to cover EL, or otherwise face a capital penalty. This move to a UL-only risk-weighted arrangement should result in the alignment of regulatory capital more closely with banks' actual economic capital requirement levels. A UL-only framework should result in banks regarding their capital base in a different light but should leave overall capital levels the same. The EL portion of risk-weighted assets is part of total eligible capital provision; and shortage in eligible provisions will be deducted in a proportion of 50% from Tier 1 capital and 50% from Tier 2 capital. So the definition of Tier 1 and Tier 2 capital has changed under Basel II; the final framework withdraws the inclusion of general loan loss reserves in Tier 2 capital and excludes expected credit losses from required capital.

Note that the BIS's desire to leave the general level of capital in the system at current levels means that a 'scaling factor' can be applied to adjust the level of capital. This scaling factor has not been determined but will be assessed based on data collected by the BIS during the parallel running period. It will then be applied to the risk-weighted asset value for credit risk.

The building blocks of the IRB approach remain as when first described – namely, the statistical measures of individual asset credit risk levels. This incorporates:

- *probability of default* (*PD*) – that is, the measure of probability that the obligor defaults over a specified time horizon;
- *loss-given-default* (*LGD*) – that is, the amount that a bank expects to incur in the event of default. A cash amount measure per asset, showing value-at-risk in the event of default;
- *exposure-at-default* (*EAD*) – this refers to bank guarantees, credit lines and liquidity lines and is the forecast amount of how much a borrower will draw upon in the event of default;

- *remaining maturity* (*M*) of an asset – on the basis that an asset with a longer remaining term-to-maturity will have a higher probability of experiencing default or other such credit event than an asset of shorter maturity.

Under the advanced IRB approach, a bank is allowed to calculate its own capital requirement using its own internal measures of PD, LGD, EAD and M. These will be calculated by the bank's internal model using historical data on each asset, plus asset-specific data. The calculation method itself is described in Basel II; however, a bank will supply its own internal data on the assets. These include the confidence level: the IRB formula is calculated based on a 99.9% confidence level and a 1-year time horizon. This means there is a 99.9% probability that the minimum amount of regulatory capital held by a bank will cover its economic losses over the next 12 months. Put simply, that means that statistically there is only a 1 in 1,000 chance that a bank's losses would erode completely its capital base, assuming that this was kept at the regulatory minimum level.

Table 9.1 shows the new risk categories for capital allocation under the new accord's IRB approach.

Basel II recognises that different types of assets behave differently, and is much more flexible than Basel I in this respect. Basel II provides specific capital calculation formulae for the following four

Table 9.1 Basel II counterparty risk weights.

Asset type	AAA to AA−	A+ to A−	BBB+ to BBB−	BB+ to BB−	B+ to B−	Below B− (including defaulted)	Unrated
Sovereigns	0	20	50	100	100	150	100
Banks, option 1[1]	20	50	100	100	100	150	100
Banks, option 2[2] > 3 months	20	50	50	100	100	150	50
Banks, option 2 < 3 months	20	20	20	50	50	150	20
Corporates	20	50	100	100	150	150	100

[1] Risk weighting based on the sovereign in which the bank is incorporated.
[2] Risk weighting based on the rating of the individual bank.

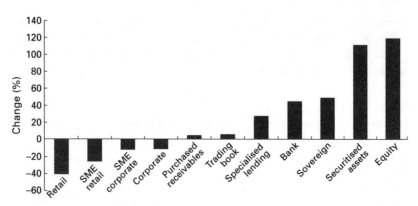

Figure 9.1   Basel II capital requirements for different asset classes: % change versus Basel I.

asset types in a banking book: corporates, commercial, real estate and retail. Different asset classes will see different capital requirements under Basel II: Figure 9.1 shows the BIS's own estimate of the change in requirements for Basel II compared with Basel I.

EXERCISES

Exercise 1

Repo versus money market alternatives

Rank the following money market instruments in order of highest return.

(a) A 12-month $ certificate of deposit (CD) paying interest at maturity at a rate of 7.25%, accruing on an act/360 basis.

(b) A 12-month PTE domestic term repo paying 7.27%, accruing on an act/365 basis.

(c) A 12-month $ repo paying interest quarterly at a rate of 7.20%, accruing on an act/360 basis.

(d) A Spanish *bono* with 1 year to maturity, a coupon of 11.00% and a price of 103.16 (accruing at act/act).

(e) A UK 1-year T-bill offered at a discount rate of 7.125%.

Exercise 2

Bond basics

A UK Government bond with a coupon of $7\frac{1}{2}$% will be redeemed at par on 15 May 2007. What is the price of the bond on 16 May 1998 if the yield to maturity is 9%?

If the semi-annual yield to maturity of a bond is 12.38%, what is:

(a) The equivalent annual yield to maturity?

(b) The equivalent quarterly yield to maturity?

The yield on a UK Government bond is 11.5% while the yield on a sterling eurobond is 11.75%. Which paper is offering the better return?

Exercise 3

A trader wishing to finance his long bond position will effect a:

(a) reverse repo transaction and pay the repo rate;
(b) repo transaction and receive the repo rate;
(c) repo transaction and pay the repo rate;
(d) reverse repo transaction and receive the repo rate.

The three main forms of delivery are, in order of safety for the cash investor:

(a) delivery repo, hold-in-custody repo and tri-party repo;
(b) tri-party repo, delivery repo and hold-in-custody repo;
(c) hold-in-custody (HIC) repo, tri-party repo and delivery repo;
(d) delivery repo, tri-party repo and hold-in-custody repo.

Which *two* of the following are correct?

As a bond becomes very special, the applicable repo rate is pushed:

(a) upwards, reducing the interest rate the dealer receives on his cash;
(b) downwards, reducing the interest rate the dealer receives on his cash;
(c) upwards, increasing the potential return for the bond lender;
(d) downwards, increasing the potential return for the bond lender.

'A spot sale and forward purchase of bonds transacted simultaneously' best describes a:

(a) repo;
(b) sell/buy-back;
(c) HIC repo;
(d) tri-party repo.

In a repo transaction the primary risk for the cash provider is the:

(a) credit risk of the counterparty;
(b) market risk of the bonds;
(c) credit risk of the bonds;
(d) intra-day settlement risk.

Exercise 4

Forward rates exercise

A bank customer asks you to fix today a rate at which he could issue a 2-year zero-coupon bond in 3 years' time. What rate do you quote? The rate quoted is the break-even rate (at which you could hedge the exposure) plus any margin. At this time let us assume that zero-coupon rates are:

1-year	6.25%
2-year	6.75%
3-year	7.00%
4-year	7.125%
5-year	7.25%

(a) Ignoring borrowing spreads over these benchmark yields, as a market maker you could cover the exposure created by borrowing funds for 5 years on a zero-coupon basis and placing these funds in the market for 3 years before lending them on to your client. Assume annual interest compounding (even if none is actually paid out during the life of the loans):

Borrowing rate for 5 years $\left[\dfrac{R_5}{100}\right] =$

Lending rate for 3 years $\left[\dfrac{R_3}{100}\right] =$

(b) The key arbitrage relationship is:

3y	known		2y	unknown	
5y		known			

The return from either investment strategy must be such that rates are arbitrage-free (i.e., the future value from either investment strategy must be equal). In our case, the 3-year and 5-year rates are known. Determine the expression for:

Total cost of funding = Total return on invesments

and solve for the 2-year interest rate 3 years forward.

Exercise 5

Repo position management

Starting the day with a flat position, you transact the following deals:

(1) £50 million repo in the 3-week at 5.375%;
(2) £30 million repo in the 1-month at 5.00% (special);
(3) a 32-day £68 million reverse repo at 5.45%.

Review your cash position and the implications for refunding and interest-rate risk, bearing in mind the following:

- you have an internal overnight roll-over limit of £30 million (net);
- your bank's economist feels more pessimistic about a rise in interest rates than most others in the market, and has recently given an internal seminar on the dangers of inflation in the UK as a result of recent increases in the level of average earnings;
- if today's RPI figures exceed market expectations, you expect a tightening of monetary policy by *at least* 0.50% very soon;
- the brokers' estimate of daily market liquidity for the next few weeks is one of low shortage, with little central bank intervention required, and hence low volatilities and rates in the overnight;
- brokers' screens indicate the following term repo rates:

O/N	5.350%–5.300%
1 week	5.390%–5.340%
2 week	5.400%–5.350%
1 month	5.410%–5.375%
2 month	5.500%–5.450%
3 month	5.670%–5.620%

- The indication for a 1v2 forward rate agreement (*FRA*) is:

    1v2 FRA   5.680%–5.630%

- The quote for the 11-day forward–forward repo in 3 weeks' time (21v32 rate) is 5.50% bid.

The book's exposure looks like this:

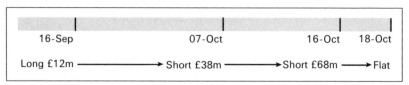

What should you do?

Remember that a book needs to be squared off such that the position is flat each night.

Discuss and come up with specific trades that you could undertake that would position the book as required and also maximise profit. It is frequently possible to deal inside interbank quotes, for various reasons including where there is an established relationship. Note that dealing at forward rates is a possibility when you wish to lock in rates based on today's yield curve (possibly because you fear rates will move against you in the future).

Exercise 6

The net basis

The gross basis is the difference between the actual price of the bond and the forward price of the bond as implied by the price of the futures contract, and represents the carrying cost of the bond. The *net basis* is the actual difference between the coupon gain and re-investment minus the carry costs (which is at the actual money market repo rate). A positive net basis represents the loss that would result from a long cash/short futures position, and therefore the theoretical gain from a short cash/long futures trade, where the actual repo rate is the reverse repo rate transacted when covering the short cash position.

Net basis is given by:

$$\left(P_d \times \left(1 + r \times \frac{Del}{36,500}\right)\right) - ((P_{fut} \times CF) + AI_{del})$$

where
P_d = Bond dirty price;
r = Repo rate;
Del = Days to delivery;
P_{fut} = Futures price;
CF = Conversion factor;
AI_{del} = Accrued interest to delivery.

Bloomberg example – US Treasury market

Settlement date	7 Dec 1998
Futures price	129-01

T 8.75% 15 May 2017   140-00
Repo rate   4.70%

Cash flows

Cash out: 7/12/98 140-00 plus accrued   = 140.531768
Cash in: 31/3/99 (129-01 × 1.0709) plus accrued = 141.4669
                                          (114 days later)
Calculate the:

(a) implied repo rate;
(b) gross basis;
(c) net basis.

ANSWERS TO EXERCISES

Exercise 1

Formulae

To roughly convert A/360 to effective annual rate:

$$E\% = Q\% \times \frac{365}{360}$$

where $E\%$ = Effective rate;
         $Q\%$ = Quoted rate.

Example 1: Quoted rate of 9% has an effective annual rate of 9.125%.

To compound up to effective annual rate:

$$E\% = \left(1 + \frac{Q\%}{n}\right)^n - 1$$

where $E\%$ = Effective rate;
         $Q\%$ = Quoted rate;
         n = Number of payments in year.

Example 2: Effective annual equivalent of 10% (quarterly) is:

$$\left(1 + \frac{0.10}{4}\right)^4 - 1 = 10.38\%$$

To calculate money market returns from present and future values:

$$R_m\% = \left(\frac{FV}{PV} - 1\right) \times \frac{B}{n}$$

where $R_m\%$ = Money market rate of return;
            FV = Future value (cash at maturity);
            PV = Present value (cash price);
            B = Day base (for money market);
            n = Number of actual days in period.

Example 3: Money market return of a 91-day T-bill at price 97.50:

$$\left(\frac{100}{97.50} - 1\right) \times \frac{360}{91} = 10.14\%$$

Example 4: Money market return of a 4% coupon, 1-year bond at price 95.45:

$$\left(\frac{104}{95.45} - 1\right) \times \frac{360}{365} = 8.83\%$$

Note both these rates are now quoted according to the conventions of their respective money market. If the day base is A/360, the effective rate will be higher (8.96% in the case of Example 2).

To convert a discount rate to an equivalent yield:

$$y\% = \frac{d\%}{1 - \left(\dfrac{d\% \times n}{B}\right)}$$

where $y\%$ = Equivalent yield;
            $d\%$ = Quoted discount interest rate;
            n = Tenor (number of days to maturity);
            B = Day base (assumed number of days in year).

Example 5: A UK T-bill with 30 days to maturity and a discount rate of 6.02% has an equivalent yield of:

$$\frac{6.02\%}{1 - \left(\dfrac{6.02\% \times 30}{365}\right)} = 6.05\%$$

Answers

The money market instruments ranked in order of highest total investment return over a 12-month period:

	Effective rate	Rank
(a) $ CD, 7.25%		
Action: multiply by 365/360	= 7.35%	4
(b) PTE repo, 7.27%		
Action: none – this is a true return	= 7.27%	5
(c) $ Repo, 7.20%		
Action: multiply by 365/360		
AND compound over four periods	= 7.51%	3
(d) *Bono*, coupon 11.00%, price 103.16		
Action: Fv (111.00)/Pv (103.16) −1	= 7.60%	2
(e) UK T-bill at 7.125% discount		
Action: use the formula supplied, or		
Action: Fv (100)/Pv (92.875) −1	= 7.67%	1

Exercise 2

Formulae

The formula for the fair price of a semi-annual paying vanilla bond is:

$$P = \frac{C}{r}\left[1 - \frac{1}{\left(1 + \frac{1}{2}r\right)^{2n}}\right] + \frac{M}{\left(1 + \frac{1}{2}r\right)^{2n}}$$

where P = Fair price of the bond;
                 C = Annual fixed coupon payment;
                 M = Par value of bond (100);
                 n = Number of complete years to maturity;
                 r = Market-determined rate of return.

Formulae for converting between semi-annual, annual and quarterly yields:

$$rm_a = \left[\left(1 + \tfrac{1}{2}rm_s\right)^2 - 1\right]$$

$$rm_s = \left[\left(1 + rm_a\right)^{\frac{1}{2}} - 1\right] \times 2$$

$$rm_a = \left[\left(1 + \tfrac{1}{4}rm_q\right)^4 - 1\right]$$

$$rm_q = \left[\left(1 + rm_a\right)^{\frac{1}{4}} - 1\right] \times 4$$

where rm_q, rm_s and rm_a are the quarterly, semi-annually and annually compounded yields to maturity.

Answers

(1) Inserting the data into the equation we obtain:

$$\frac{£7.5}{0.09}\left[1 - \frac{1}{[1 + \frac{1}{2}(0.09)]^{18}}\right] + \frac{100}{[1 + \frac{1}{2}(0.09)]^{18}} = 83.33\left[1 - \frac{1}{2.208\,48}\right]$$

$$+ \frac{100}{2.208\,48}$$

$$= £45.598 + £45.28$$

$$= £90.878$$

The fair price of the bond is £90.878, composed of the present value of the stream of coupon payments (£45.598) and the present value of the return of the principal (£45.28).

(2) A semi-annual yield of 12.38% implies:

(a) an annual yield of:

$$rm_a = \{[1 + 0.5(0.1238)]^2 - 1\} = 0.1276(12.76\%)$$

b) while an annual yield of 12.76% implies a quarterly yield of:

$$rm_q = \left[(1 + 0.1276)^{\frac{1}{4}} - 1\right] \times 4 = 0.1219(12.19\%)$$

3. The equivalent annual yield on the gilt is 11.83% so it offers the better return.

Exercise 3

Answers

(c)
(d) In order of safety: delivery repo, tri-party repo, HIC repo.
(b) and (d)
(b)
(a) But, debatable!

Exercise 4

Forward rates answer

(a) From the current zero-coupon curve we know the following:

Borrowing rate for 5 years $\left[\dfrac{R_5}{100}\right] = 0.0725$

Lending rate for 3 years $\left[\dfrac{R_3}{100}\right] = 0.0700$

(b) Our knowledge of forward rates and the fact that derived rates must be arbitrage-free tell us that:

Total cost of funding = Total return on invesments

$$(1 + R_5)^5 = (1 + R_3)^3 \times (1 + R_{3\times5})^2$$

$$(1 + R_{3\times5})^2 = \frac{(1 + 0.0725)^5}{(1 + 0.0700)^3}$$

$$(1 + R_{3\times5}) = \sqrt{\left[\frac{(1 + 0.0725)^5}{(1 + 0.0700)^3}\right]}$$

$$R_{3\times5} = \sqrt{\left[\frac{(1 + 0.0725)^5}{(1 + 0.0700)^3}\right]} - 1$$

Therefore, the forward rate quoted to the customer (excluding any spread) is:

$$R_{3\times5} = 7.63\%$$

Exercise 5

Repo position management

Investing early surplus

From a cash management point of view, you have a £12 million surplus from 16/9 up to 7/10. This needs to be invested. You can negotiate a 5.31% GC reverse repo with the market for overnight, and 5.35% for a term of 1 week to 5.38% for 1 month.

The overnight roll is the most flexible but offers a worse rate, and you expect the O/N rate to remain both low and stable due to forecasts of low shortages.

However, it may make sense from an interest-rate risk point of view. If you agree with your economist, you should be able to benefit from rolling at higher rates soon – possibly in the next 3 weeks. So, you may not want to lock in a term rate now, and the overnight roll would match your view. However, it exposes you to lower rates, if your view is wrong, which will limit your positive funding spread. The market itself appears neutral about rate changes in the next month, but factors in a rise thereafter.

The forward 'gap'

Looking forward, you are currently projected to exceed your £30 million overnight position limit on 7/10, when the refunding requirement is £38 million. The situation gets worse on 16/10 (for 2 days) when the refunding requirement is £68 million. You need to fix a term repo deal before those dates to carry you over until 18/10 when the funding position reverts to 0.

A repo from 7/10 to 18/10 of, say, £40 million will reduce the rollover requirement to within limit. (Or you may fix it precisely at £38m.)

But, given that interest rates will rise, should you wait until the 7th to deal that repo? Not if you are firm in your view. You may be paying as much as 5.91% or higher for your funding (after the 0.50% rate rise). So, it would be better to transact now a forward starting repo to cover the period, thus locking in the benefits obtainable from today's yield curve. The market rate for a 21 × 32-day repo is quoted at 5.50%. This reflects the market's consensus that rates may rise in about a month's time. However, your own expectation is of a larger rise, hence your own logic suggests you should indeed transact the forward repo. This strategy will pay dividends if your view is right in that it limits your funding loss.

An alternative means of protecting the interest-rate risk alone is to *buy* a 1v2-month FRA for 5.68%. This does not exactly match the gap, but should act as an effective hedge. If there is a rate rise, you gain from the FRA profit. Of course, you still need to square your cash position.

Should you deal before or after the inflation announcement? That is of course your view and the essence of trading...!

Exercise 6

The net basis answers

Implied repo rate:

$$100 \times \left(\frac{360}{114}\right) \times \left(\frac{141.4669}{140.531\,768} - 1\right) = \mathbf{2.101\,339\%}$$

Gross basis:

$$140.00 - 138.179\,5656 = \mathbf{1.8204}$$

Net basis:

$$\left[140.531\,768 \times \left(1 + 4.7 \times \frac{114}{36,000}\right)\right] - 141.4669 = \mathbf{1.156\,449}$$

CASE STUDY:
ABC BANK plc

. . . .

We now present a case study of four different repo trades from the point of view of a repo market-making bank, the hypothetical ABC Bank plc. Carry out the calculations to enable you to complete the trade tickets. Answers are given at the end.

Repo Case Study

The date is Tuesday, 4 January 2000. The following represents the repo desk of ABC Bank plc. The pages show customer requests for repos and reverse repos using different trade structures. Settlement is next business day, Wednesday 5 January 2000, and apart from the price quote in trade 1, assume there are no bid–offer spreads.

TRADE 1

The treasurer of Commercial Bank plc requests :

The quote is:
bid–offer
5 9/16%–5 1/2%

• "The price in 1 month GC?"

• "It's nine-sixteenths, a half"

• "OK, I'll take £50 million at a half."

(Note: Back office supplies collateral of gilt 5% 2004)

TRADE 2

Henry Marshall Securities calls, looking for a bond that is in strong demand in the repo market...

"I'm looking to borrow £30 million nominal of the gilt five-threes 09 on a buy-sell back basis up to 31 March. Where do you offer them?"

Is this for the basis? I'm afraid 5%–the figure is the best I can do.

"Okay, done."

... lets check clearer CDs...

NOTE: Due to lack of signed counterparty documentation in place, this trade is carried out as a sell-buy back!

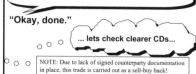

TRADE 3

Quanto Asset Management calls, wanting to fund a US
Treasury position with sterling:

"Where do you bid for $100 million nominal of Treasuries for 7 days versus sterling?"

I can do it at 4.90%, need a 2% haircut.

"Okay, done."

TRADE 4

Your trader thinks a certain gilt is overpriced
and has just shorted it. You need to cover the
position and call Rasheed Pension Fund, who
only do securities lending.....

" I'd like to borrow £100 million of the 7Qs 07 for 14 days. What about some 6-and-a half's 03 as collateral and a fee of 20bp?"

You can have them loan fee is 40 bp
plus a 5% margin.

RELEVANT RATES

MONEY MARKET RATES

GBP interbank–1 w	4.95%	GBP interbank o/n	4.70%
GBP interbank–1 mo	5.65%	GBP interbank t/n	4.75%
UK T-Bill (1 mo)	5.20%	UK T-Bill (3 mo)	5.40%
AA+ name CD (3m tenor)	6.00%	AA name 1m CD	5.60%
Repo 1 week GC	4.90%		
Repo 1 month GC	5.50%		
Repo to 31 March GC	5.75%		

EXCHANGE RATES
£1 = $1.63
BONDS

	Clean Prices	Accrued
UK gilt 5% 2004	95.25	29 days
UK gilt 5.75% 2009	100.79	29 days
US Treasury 6 1/8% 2001	99.59375	5 days
UK gilt 7 1/4% 2007	107.84	29 days
UK gilt 6 1/2% 2003	100.42	29 days

. . . .

Trade 1

ABC Bank plc

ABC repo trading ticket

Counterparty ___Commercial Bank plc___

Trade date _____ **Settlement date** _____

Collateral _____ **Nominal amount**_____

Repo rate_____

Term _____days (From _____ To _____)

Note 5 February 2000 is a Saturday!

Clean price _____

(CREST Reference price – given)

Accrued _____

Note: the UK gilt market uses act/act for accrued interest The coupon dates are 7 June and 7 December.

Dirty price_____

Settlement amount (wired amount) _____

Repo interest _____

(Repo interest day-count: act/365)

Termination money _____

---

1. What sort of yield is this investor receiving compared with Libor?
2. How does the repo rate compare with the return on unsecured paper?
3. Give some reasons why Commercial Bank's treasurer might make this investment rather than deposit the funds in a bank or purchase a T-bill?
4. What is the running yield on the 5% 2004? If you regard the trade as ABC plc in effect funding its position in this stock, what is the funding gain/loss during the 1-month period?

Trade 2

ABC Bank plc

ABC buy/sell-back trading ticket

Counterparty _Henry Marshall Securities_

Trade date _____ **Settlement date** _____

Collateral UKT $5\frac{3}{4}$% 2009 **Nominal amount** _____

Repo rate _____

Term _____ days (**From** _____ **To** _____)

Clean price _____

Accrued _____

(Act/act; coupon dates 7 June and 7 December)

Dirty price _____

Settlement amount (wired amount) _____

Repo interest _____

Termination amount _____

Forward dirty price _____

Forward accrued _____

Forward clean price _____

---

1. What is the premium on the equivalent maturity GC rate?
2. By investing the proceeds in CDs, what total profit in basis points will you earn over the 3-month period (on an annualised basis), and what sort of risk are you, the repo dealer, exposing yourself to?
3. How could you have invested the proceeds for a risk-free return?

Trade 3

ABC Bank plc

ABC reverse repo trading ticket

Counterparty <u>Quanto Asset Management</u>

Trade date _____ **Settlement date** _____

Collateral _____ **Nominal Amount** _____

Repo rate _____

Term _____ **days (From** _____ **To** _____)

Clean price _____

US daycount method is act/act; coupon dates 30 Jun, 31 Dec.

Accrued _____

Dirty price _____

Gross settlement amount in USD _____

Net settlement amount after haircut in USD _____

(use Bloomberg method)

Net settlement amount (wired amount) in GBP _____

GBP repo interest _____

GBP termination money _____

---

1. What is Quanto Asset Management's cost of funds compared with what it would have paid with an unsecured borrowing?
2. Who is over-collateralised? Are there any other risks for the cash lender?

Trade 4

ABC Bank plc

ABC stock loan ticket

Counterparty ___Rasheed Pension Fund___

Trade date _____ Settlement date _____

Bonds borrowed _____ Nominal amount_____

Fee_____

Term _____days (From _____ To _____)

Clean price _____

Accrued _____

(Gilt is act/act; coupon dates 7 June and 7 December)

Dirty price _____

Loan value _____

Stock loan fee payable _____

- -

Clean price of collateral (UKT $6\frac{1}{2}$% 2003) _____

Accrued of collateral _____

Dirty price of collateral _____

Value of collateral required, given 5% margin _____

Nominal of collateral required _____

REPO CASE STUDY ANSWERS

Trade 1

ABC Bank plc

ABC repo trading ticket

Counterparty Commercial Bank plc

Trade date 4 January 2000 **Settlement date** 5 January 2000

Collateral UKT 5% 2004 **Nominal amount** £50,000,000

Repo rate $5\frac{1}{2}$%

Term 33 days **(From** 5/1/00 **To** 7/2/00)

Clean price 95.25

Accrued 0.3961749 (5.00/2 × 29/183) or (5.00 × 29/366)

Dirty price 95.6461749

Settlement amount (wired amount) £47,823,087

Repo interest £237,805.21 (£47,823,087 × $5\frac{1}{2}$% × 33/365)

Termination money £48,060,892.21

---

1. Commercial Bank plc is earning Libor −15 bps, but with AAA security against its investment.
2. It is 10 bps lower (the CD is at 5.60%). Repo investments usually yield about the same or less than investment grade unsecured paper, government bond repo always less due to the quality of security.
3. Investors often have a limited amount of credit lines for unsecured investment counterparties. In addition, the repo offers 30-bps higher return than the T-Bill for what is still essentially government risk. Finally, buying paper can have mark-to-market implications and associated interest-rate risk, which Commercial Bank plc may not desire, and which requires different monitoring and settlement systems.
4. The running yield is 5.227% (this is an approximation and uses the dirty price). In effect, the net funding on this position is a loss of 0.273% for the term of the repo, obtained by subtracting the repo rate paid to Commercial Bank from the running yield on the bond.

Trade 2

ABC Bank plc

ABC buy/sell-back trading ticket

Counterparty Henry Marshall Securities

Trade date 4 January 2000 **Settlement date** 5 January 2000

Collateral UKT $5\frac{3}{4}$% 2009 **Nominal amount** £30m

Repo rate 5%

Term 86 days (**From** 5/1/00 **To** 31/3/00)

Clean price 100.79

Accrued 0.455 601 09 (5.75/2 × 29/183) or (5.75 × 29/366)

Dirty price 101.245 601

Settlement amount £30,373,680.33 (101.245 601% × 30,000,000)

Repo interest £357,826.92 (5% × £30,373,680.33 × 86/365)

Termination amount £30,731,507.25 (£30,373,680.33 + £357,826.92)

Forward dirty price 102.438 3575 (termination money/nominal)

Forward accrued 1.806 6940 (5.75/2 × 115/183) or (5.75 × 115/366)

Forward clean price 100.631 664 (dirty price minus accrued)

---

1. 5.75 − 5.00; that is, 75 basis points.
2. By investing the proceeds in high-grade CDs yielding 6.00%, you will earn 100 basis points (6.00%–5.00%). You are, however, exposing yourself to some credit risk (however small!).
3. For a virtually risk-free gain, you could have invested the cash proceeds in another Treasury repo (secured by general collateral) of the same maturity. The repo investment, at 5.75%, would earn you a 75-bps profit.

Trade 3

ABC Bank plc

ABC reverse repo trading ticket

Counterparty Quanto Asset Management

Trade date 4 January 2000 **Settlement date** 5 January 2000

Collateral UST $6\frac{1}{8}$% 2001 **Nominal amount** USD 100m

Repo rate 4.90% (STG)

Term 7 days (From 5/1/00 **To** 12/1/00)

Clean price 99.593 75

Accrued 0.084 1346 (6.125/2 × 5/182) or (6.125 × 5/364)

Dirty price 99.677 8846

Gross settlement amount USD 99,677,884.62

Net settlement amount (after 2% haircut) USD 97,723,416.29 (/1.02)

Net wired settlement amount in GBP @ 1.63 £59,953,016.13

Repo interest £56,339.41 (£59,953,016.13 × 4.90% × 7/365)

GBP termination money £60,009,355.54

---

1. The repo market has allowed Quanto to borrow in sterling at a rate below the cost of unsecured borrowing in the money market (4.95%). The investor could have chosen to borrow in USD or another major currency, with similar savings.
2. You, the repo dealer, are 'over-collateralised' by the difference between the value of the bonds (in £) and the loan proceeds (2%). A rise in USD yields or a fall in the USD exchange rate value will adversely affect the value of the bonds, causing you to be under-collateralised. Quanto needs to be prepared to either deliver additional collateral or reduce the loan balance in this event.

Trade 4

ABC Bank plc

ABC stock loan ticket

Counterparty Rasheed Pension Fund

Trade date 4 January 2000 **Settlement date** 5 January 2000

Bonds borrowed UKT $7\frac{1}{4}$% 2007 **Nominal amount** £100m

Fee 40 basis points

Term 14 days (From 5/1/00 **To** 19/1/00)

Clean price 107.84

Accrued 0.574 453 55 [(7.25/2) × 29/183] or [7.25 × 29/366]

Dirty price 108.414 453 55

Loan value £108,414,453.55

Stock loan fee payable £16,633.45 (note comments below)

- -

Clean price of collateral (UKT $6\frac{1}{2}$% **2003)** 100.42

Accrued of collateral 0.515 0273 [6.25/2 × 29/183]

Dirty price of collateral 100.935 0273

Market value of collateral required, given 5% margin: £113,835,176.23

Nominal amount of collateral required £112,780,646 [/1.009 350 273]

In a classic repo or buy/sell-back, the implicit cost of holding the short position is the difference between the repo rate for general collateral and the 'special' rate paid in exchange for borrowing the specific desired issue. In the case of stock loan, the cost is explicit, in the fee of 40 bps. The cash charge is 40 bps of the loan value over the 14 days, or £16,633.45.

Note that, in reality, in the gilt market the stock loan fee (here 40 bps) is calculated on the daily mark-to-market stock price, automatically within CREST-CGO, so the final charge is not known until termination. Within the Eurobond market – for example, in Clearstream – the fee on the initial loan value is taken, and adjustments are made only in the case of large movements in price.

GLOSSARY

. . . .

Glossary of terms used in repo markets.

Agent   The gilt repo code uses the term 'agent' to cover participants in the market such as fund managers and custodians who undertake repo transactions on behalf of (principal) clients.

All-in price   *See* **Dirty price**.

BMA (TBMA)   The Bond Market Association (previously the Public Securities Association). A US-based organisation which developed the market standard documentation for repo in the US domestic market, and which developed with ICMA the Global Master Repurchase Agreement (*GMRA*).

BMA/ICMA Global Master Repurchase Agreement   Developed by BMA and ICMA jointly, this is the market standard documentation for non-dollar repo markets. A revised edition was issued in November 1995. The Gilt Repo Legal Agreement is an amended version of the revised edition (through the inclusion of a Part 2 to its Annex I and modified by a side letter in connection with the upgrade of the CGO service in 1997) designed to meet the needs of the gilt repo market.

Basis risk   A form of market risk that arises whenever one kind of risk exposure is hedged with an instrument that behaves in a similar, but not necessarily identical way. For instance, a bank trading desk may use 3-month interest rate futures to hedge its commercial paper or euronote programme. Although eurocurrency rates, to which futures prices respond, are well-correlated with commercial paper rates they do not always move in lock step. If therefore commercial paper rates move by 10 basis points but futures prices dropped by only 7 basis points, the 3-bps gap would be the basis risk.

Bid   The repo rate that the cash investor demands from the seller to 'bid' for stock – that is, lend the cash. This is the same terminology and price quote as for CDs.

Broker   An intermediary who brokes repo, either on a matched principal or name-passing basis.

Bulldog   Sterling domestic bonds issued by non-UK domiciled borrowers. These bonds – under a similar arrangement to gilts – are settled via the Central Gilts Office.

Buy/sell-back or sell/buy-back   Transactions which are not specifically repo but have the same effect and intent and which consist of a simultaneous matching purchase and sale of the same quantity of securities for different value dates. The UK's Gilt Repo Code recommends that buy/sell-backs should only be carried out under a master agreement with the same protections as those given in the Gilt Repo Legal Agreement.

Calling the mark   The process of calling for margin to be re-instated following a mark-to-market revaluation of a repo transaction.

Central Gilts Office   The office of the Bank of England which runs the computer-based settlement system for gilt-edged securities and certain other securities (mostly **Bulldogs**) for which the Bank acts as registrar.

CBOT   Chicago Board of Trade, one of the two futures exchanges in Chicago, USA and one of the largest in the world.

CGO reference prices   Daily prices of gilt-edged and other securities held in CGO which are used by CGO in various processes, including revaluing stock loan transactions, calculating total consideration in a repo transaction and DBV assembly.

Closing leg   A repo involves a pair of trades in the same security, one for a near value date and the other for a value date in the future. The closing leg refers to the second of these. *See* **Opening leg**.

Collateral   A general term used in the market to cover any securities exchanged in a repo transaction, both initially and subsequently during the period before the repo matures. Under the BMA/ICMA and Gilt Repo Legal Agreements, full title to collateral passes from one party to another, the party obtaining title being obliged to deliver back *equivalent* securities.

Day-count   The convention used to calculate accrued interest on bonds and interest on cash. For UK gilts the convention changed to actual/actual from actual/365 on 1 November 1998. For cash the convention in sterling markets is actual/365.

DBV (delivery by value)   A mechanism whereby a CGO member may borrow from or lend money to another CGO member against overnight gilt collateral. The CGO system automatically selects and delivers securities to a specified aggregate value on the basis of the previous night's CGO reference prices; equivalent securities are returned the following day. The DBV functionality allows the giver and taker of collateral to specify the classes of security to include within the DBV. The options are: all classes of security held within CGO, including strips and bulldogs; coupon bearing gilts and bulldogs; coupon bearing gilts and strips; only coupon bearing gilts.

Delivery versus payment (DVP)   The simultaneous exchange of securities and cash. The assured payment mechanism of the CGO achieves the same protection.

Dirty price   The price of a bond including accrued interest. Also known as the 'all-in' price.

Duration weighting   The process of using the modified duration value for bonds to calculate the exact nominal holdings in a spread position. This is necessary because £1 million nominal of a 2-year bond is not equivalent to £1 million of, say, a 5-year bond. The modified duration value of the 5-year bond will be higher, indicating that its 'basis point value' (BPV) will be greater, and that therefore £1 million worth of this bond represents greater sensitivity to a move in interest rates (risk). As another example, consider a fund manager holding £10 million of 5-year bonds. The fund manager wishes to switch into a holding of 2-year bonds with the same overall risk position. The BPVs of the bonds are 0.041 583 and 0.022 898, respectively. The ratio of the BPVs are 0.041 583/0.022 898 = 1.816. The fund manager therefore needs to switch into £10m × 1.816 = £18.160 million of the 2-year bond.

Equivalent securities   A term used in repo to denote that the securities returned must be of identical issue (and tranche, where relevant) and nominal value to those repoed.

Ex-dividend (xd) date   A bond's record date for the payment of coupons. The coupon payment will be made to the person who is the registered holder of the stock on the xd date. For gilts this is seven working days before the coupon date.

General collateral (GC) Securities, which are not 'special', used as collateral against cash borrowing. A repo buyer will accept GC at any time that a specific stock is not quoted as required in the transaction. In the gilts market GC includes DBVs.

Hold-in-custody (HIC) repo A repo in which the party who receives cash does not deliver the securities to the counterparty but segregates them in an internal account for the benefit of the cash provider.

Initial margin The excess – either of cash over the value of securities or of the value of securities over cash – in a repo transaction at the time it is executed and, subsequently, after margin calls.

ICMA The International Capital Market Association (previously the International Securities Market Association). This association designed with the PSA (now renamed the Bond Market Association) the BMA/ICMA Global Master Repurchase Agreement.

Libor The London Interbank Offered Rate, the rate for all major currencies up to a 1-year term, set at 11:00 hours each day by the British Bankers Association.

LIFFE The London International Financial Futures Exchange, the largest futures exchange in Europe.

Manufactured dividend The payment (of an amount equal to the gross coupon on the security concerned) which the acquirer of the security in a repo is generally contractually obliged to make to the other party when the acquirer receives a coupon on a security which passes the ex-dividend date during the course of the repo.

Margin call A request following marking-to-market of a repo transaction for the initial margin to be reinstated or where no initial margin has been taken to restore the cash/securities ratio to parity.

Mark-to-market In repo transactions the act of revaluing securities to current market values. Such revaluations should include both coupon accrued on the securities outstanding and interest accrued on the cash; it should also take into account any coupon which passes its ex-dividend date during the life of the repo.

Matched book This refers to the matching by a repo trader of securities repoed in and out. It carries no implications that the trader's position is 'matched' in terms of exposure – for example, to short-term interest rates.

Offer The repo rate that the seller is willing to pay on cash received to 'offer' the stock – that is, take the cash

Opening leg The first half of a repo transaction. *See* **Closing leg**.

Open repo A repo trade with no fixed maturity date, with the daily possibility of terminating the repo or re-fixing its terms or substituting collateral.

OTC Over the counter. Strictly speaking, any transaction not conducted on a registered stock exchange. Trades conducted via the telephone between banks and contracts such as FRAs and (non-exchange traded) options are said to be 'over-the-counter' instruments.

Principle A party to a repo transaction who acts on their own behalf.

Refer The practice whereby a trader instructs a broker to put 'under reference' any prices or rates he has quoted to him, meaning that they are no longer 'firm' and the broker must refer to the trader before he can trade on the price initially quoted.

Repo rate The return earned on a repo transaction expressed as an interest rate on the cash side of the transaction.

Repo (reverse repo) to maturity A repo or reverse repo where the security repoed matures on the same day as the closing leg.

Roll To renew a repo trade at its maturity.

Special A security which for any reason is sought after in the repo market, thereby enabling any holder of the security to earn incremental income (in excess of GC)

through lending them via a repo transaction. The repo rate for a special will be below the GC rate, as this is the rate the borrower of the cash is paying in return for supplying the special bond as collateral.

Strip   A zero-coupon bond which is produced by separating a standard coupon-bearing bond into its constituent principal and interest components.

TBMA   Alternative abbreviation for BMA (Bond Market Association). *See* **BMA**.

Term repo   Repo trades (of a maturity over 1 day) with a fixed maturity date.

Tri-party repo   A repo in which an independent agent bank or clearing house oversees a standard two-party repo transaction. The responsibilities of the tri-party agent include maintaining acceptable and adequate collateral and overall maintenance of the outstanding repo trades.

Variation margin   The band agreed between the parties to a repo transaction at the outset within which the value of the collateral may fluctuate before triggering a right to call for cash or securities to re-instate the initial margin on the repo transaction.

TECHNICAL
APPENDICES

....

APPENDIX A   DURATION

An important concept in the bond markets is that of duration. We can define duration as the weighted average time until the receipt of cash flows from an instrument, where the weights are the present values of the cash flows. More formally we can write:

$$D = \frac{\displaystyle\sum_{t=1}^{n} \frac{tC_t}{(1+r)^t}}{P} \qquad (A.1)$$

where D = Duration;
         P = Price of the bond;
         C_t = Cash flow at time t;
         r = Yield.

In the case of a zero-coupon bond there is only one cash flow, the payment at maturity. Therefore, for zero-coupon bonds the duration is always equal to the maturity of the bond. Consider now a 10% 2-year bond yielding 10% today: the cash flows are £10 in 1 year's time and £110 in 2 years' time. Viewed as two zero-coupon bonds the cash flows would now be a 1-year zero of £10 and a 2-year zero of £110. The duration of the combined package will be the average duration of the two bonds weighted by the size of the bond. Since we are measuring the duration today it is sensible to weight the two bonds in terms of today's money in present value terms. Since the bond is a 10% bond and we are valuing it at a yield of 10% the price is par, or 100. So the duration calculation is:

$$\frac{(1 \times 9.0909 + 2 \times 90.0909)}{100} = 1.909$$

This incidentally illustrates the point that for a coupon-bearing bond the duration is always less than for the corresponding zero-coupon bond. The 2-year coupon-bearing bond has a duration of 1.91 years; the zero would have a duration of 2 years.

Duration is an important concept because *modified duration* (defined as Duration/(1 + r) where r is the redemption yield on the bond) measures the sensitivity of the bond's price to changes in the yield curve. This can be seen by drawing a chart of the bond's price at different levels of yield. The resulting slope of this line is the bond's modified duration. The proof for this follows:

$$\text{Price of bond } (P) = \sum_{t=1}^{n} \frac{C_t}{(1+r)^t}$$

$$\text{Duration } (D) = \frac{\displaystyle\sum_{t=1}^{n} \frac{tC_t}{(1+r)^t}}{P}$$

Now we differentiate P with respect to r:

$$\frac{dP}{dY} = -\sum_{t=1}^{n} tC_t(1+r)^{-t-1}$$

Multiply by $(1+r)$:

$$(1+r)\frac{dP}{dY} = -\sum_{t=1}^{n} tC_t(1+r)^{-t}$$

Divide by P:

$$\frac{dP}{dY}\frac{1+r}{P} = -\sum_{t=1}^{n} \frac{tC_t}{(1+r)^t P} = -D$$

If we define modified duration (MD) as $D/(1+r)$ then:

$$-\frac{dP}{dY}\frac{1}{P} = MD$$

Thus, modified duration measures the proportionate impact on the price of a bond of a change in yield; the sign is negative because rising yields result in lower bond prices. For example, if modified duration is 5.1 and yield rises by 1%, the bond price falls by 5.1%.

APPENDIX B   BASIS TRADING AND
THE CTD BOND

There are two competing definitions for the cheapest-to-deliver
(*CTD*) issue which usually but not always identify the same issue
as 'cheapest' – namely, (i) the issue with the highest implied repo
rate, known as the IRR method, and (ii) the issue with the lowest net
basis (basis method). Most academic literature uses the first definition, whereas market practitioners often argue that the net basis
method should be used since it measures the actual profit & loss
(*p&l*) for a 'real world' trade. We define net basis below.

> **Net basis**   The gross basis adjusted for net carry. Net carry is
> actual coupon income and re-investment less borrowing
> expense, which is at the security's actual repo (money market)
> rate. Net basis is the true 'economic basis'. A positive value
> represents a *loss* or net cost to the long cash/short futures
> position. Net basis is the expected *profit* for the short cash/long
> futures position (where actual repo is the reverse repo rate). The
> opposite is true for negative net basis values. For example, if
> gross basis for a US Treasury bond is 5 ticks (32nds of a point)
> and net basis is 2 ticks, the p&l for a long cash/short futures
> trade is a loss of 2 ticks.

It is up to the individual to decide on which method to use as the
basis for analysis. For example, Bloomberg terminals use the IRR
method. It is accepted that the IRP method is appropriate to the cash-
and-carry investor seeking maximum return per pound invested. The
main area of disagreement regards those cases where an arbitrageur
finances (repoes) the cash side of the trade and the net basis measures
his resulting profit or loss. In a Bloomberg analysis this net basis
is presented as percentage points of par (the same units as price),
although some practitioners express it as p&l per million bonds. It is
primarily because the net basis is per par amount rather than per
pound invested that the two methods occasionally identify different
'cheapest' issues. Note that in practice net basis will always be a loss,
otherwise traders would arbitrage an infinite amount of any issue
with a profitable net basis. Therefore, the basis method identifies the
issue which has the *smallest loss* per million as the cheapest issue.

The only reason a trader is willing to accept this guaranteed loss is
that he doesn't intend to follow through exactly with this trade to

maturity. Being long of the basis – that is, short futures – essentially gives the trader numerous delivery and trading options; the cost of these is the net basis that the trader pays. In effect, the trader is buying options for the cost of the net basis. The number of options he buys is indicated by the *conversion factor* since that is the hedge factor for the cheapest issue. Therefore, the cost per option is the net basis divided by the conversion factor. When ranked by net basis per contract (i.e., divided by the conversion factor), the cheapest by this method invariably agrees with the IRP method.

The formula for the calculation of the implied repo rate for a bond with no or one interim coupon is shown as Equation (A.2), which states:

$$\frac{\text{Cost to purchase}}{\text{and finance bond}} = \frac{\text{Coupon and}}{\text{re-invested earnings}} + \frac{\text{Amount received from}}{\text{contract delivery}}$$

$$(P + AI_1)\left(1 + \frac{rD_1}{365}\right) = C\left(1 + \frac{rD_2}{365}\right) \qquad + (DP + A_2)$$

Re-arranging for r we obtain:

$$r = \frac{DP + A_2 - (P + A_1) + C}{(P + A_1)(D_1/365) - C(D_2/365)} \qquad \text{(A.2)}$$

where
r = Implied repo rate (as a decimal);
P = Bond purchase clean price;
A_1 = Accrued interest at the time of purchase;
A_2 = Accrued interest on the bond on futures delivery day;
D_1 = Days from purchase settlement date to futures delivery;
D_2 = Days from interim coupon receipt to futures delivery;
C = Actual interim coupon received (is 0 if no coupon received)
DP = Delivery price (Conversion factor × Futures price).

APPENDIX C   VOLATILITY

Practitioners working in capital markets operations and textbooks written on the subject often make references to market and instrument *volatility*. Option traders also speak of *implied volatility*. Implied volatility is one of the inputs to the market standard formula used for calculating the price of an option; it cannot be measured directly as it refers to market movements in the future. Historic volatility refers to market movements that have already occurred.

The distribution of asset prices is assumed to follow a log-normal distribution, because the logarithm of the prices is normally distributed (we assume log-normal rather than normal distribution to allow for the fact that prices cannot – as could be the case in a normal distribution – have negative values): the range of possible prices starts at 0 and cannot assume a negative value. Returns are defined as the logarithm of the price relatives and are assumed to follow the normal distribution such that:

$$\ln\left(\frac{S_t}{S_0}\right) \sim N(\mu t, \sigma\sqrt{t})$$

where S_0 = Price at time 0;
         S_t = Price at time t;
$N(m, s)$ = Random variable with mean m and standard deviation s;
         μ = Annual rate of return;
         σ = Annualised standard deviation of returns;

and the symbol $\sim$ means 'is distributed according to'.

Volatility is defined in the equation above as the annualised standard deviation of returns. This definition does not refer to the variability of the prices directly but to the variability of the returns that generate these prices. Price relatives are calculated from the ratio of successive closing prices. Returns are then calculated according to the following equation as the logarithm of the price relatives:

$$\text{Return} = \ln\left(\frac{S_{t+1}}{S_t}\right)$$

where S_t = Market price at time t;
         S_{t+1} = Price one period later.

The mean and standard deviation of returns follow standard statistical techniques using the following formula:

$$\mu = \sum_{i=1}^{N} \frac{x_i}{N} \quad \text{and} \quad \sigma = \sqrt{\sum_{i=1}^{N} \frac{(x - \mu)^2}{N - 1}}$$

where x_i = ith price relative;
N = Total number of observations.

This gives a standard deviation or volatility of daily price returns. To convert this to an annual figure, it is necessary to multiply it by the square root of the number of working days in a year, normally taken to be 250.

ABBREVIATIONS

. . . .

ABN	Asset Backed loan Note
ABS	Asset Backed Securities
ALB	Asset Liability Management
BBA	British Bankers Association
BIS	Bank for International Settlements
BMA	Bond Market Association
BoE	Bank of England
bp, bps	Basis point(s)
CAD	Capital Adequacy Directive
CD	Certificate of Deposit
CDO	Collateralised Debt Obligation
CGO	Central Gilts Office
CMBS	Commercial Mortgage Backed Security
CP	Commercial Paper
CSFB	Credit Suisse First Boston
CTD	Cheapest To Deliver
DBV	Delivery By Value
DVP	Delivery Versus Payment
EAD	Exposure At Default
ECU	European Currency Unit (former term for 'euro')
EDSP	Exchange Delivery Settlement Price
EL	Expected Loss
EURIBOR, Euribor	EURo InterBank Offered Rate
FRA	Forward Rate Agreement
FRN	Floating Rate Note
FV	Future Value
GC	General Collateral

GEMM	Gilt Edged Market Maker
GESLA	Gilt Edged Stock Lending Agreement
GMRA	Global Master Repurchase Agreement
HIC	Hold In Custody
ICMA	International Capital Markets Association
IRB	Internal Risk Based
IRR	Implied Repo Rate
ISDA	International Swap Dealers Association
ISMA	International Securities Market Association
LGD	Loss Given Default
LIBID, Libid	London Interbank BID rate
LIBOR, Libor	London InterBank Offered Rate
LIFFE	London International Financial Futures Exchange
M	Remaining Maturity of an asset
MBS	Mortgage Backed Securities
MRA	Master Repurchase Agreement
NPV	Net Present Value
OECD	Organisation for Economic Cooperation and Development
O/N	Overnight
OSLA	International Stock Lenders Association
OTC	Over The Counter
PD	Probability of Default
PSA	Public Securities Association
PTE	Portuguese Treasury security
PV	Present Value
RMBS	Residential Mortgage Backed Securities
RPI	Retail Price Index
RTGS	Real Time Gross Settlement System
SEMB	Stock Exchange Money Broker
SPV	Special Purpose Vehicle
T-bill	Treasury bill
TBMA	The Bond Market Association
TRS	Total Return Swap
UL	Unexpected Loss
YTM	Yield To Maturity

INDEX

Other titles by the author

....

Corporate Bond Markets: Instruments and Applications,
  John Wiley & Sons, 2005.

The Money Markets Handbook: A Practitioner's Guide,
  John Wiley & Sons, 2005.

*Structured Credit Products: Credit Derivatives and Synthetic
  Securitisation*, John Wiley & Sons, 2004.

Advanced Fixed Income Analysis, Elsevier, 2004.

Handbook of European Fixed Income Securities (editor, with
  Frank Fabozzi), John Wiley & Sons, 2004.

Analysing and Interpreting the Yield Curve, John Wiley & Sons,
  2004.

The Gilt-Edged Market, Butterworth-Heinemann, 2003.

Derivative Instruments (with Brian Eales), Butterworth-
  Heinemann, 2003.

The Repo Handbook, Butterworth-Heinemann, 2002.

Capital Market Instruments: Analysis and Valuation, FT Prentice
  Hall, 2001.

Bond Market Securities, FT Prentice Hall, 2001.

The Bond and Money Markets: Strategy, Trading, Analysis,
  Butterworth-Heinemann, 2001.